Bringing the Professional and Academic Worlds Together: A Theatrical Memoir

by

Richard G. Fallon

Designer and Typesetter: Karen Towson Wells
Typeface: Book Antiqua
Printer and binder: Rose Printing Company

Library of Congress Number: 2004113412

ISBN 1-889574-20-1

Sentry Press
424 East Call Street
Tallahassee, Florida 32301-7693

Dedication

To my Partner, Suzanne Bowkett Fallon

and

*Our daughter, Diane Elizabeth Tomasi
her husband, Thomas Tomasi
her children,
Julia Tomasi, Rosanne Tomasi, and Corinne Tomasi*

*Our son, Rick Fallon
his wife, Sharon Fallon
his children,
Alexander Fallon and Patrick Fallon*

TABLE OF CONTENTS

PREFACE

Now, I doubt that many of you know me, because I am not famous. If you are from Florida State University, or were in one of my classes, you might remember me. However, that is not the point of this memoir.

I promised Helen Hayes the last time I was with her that I would not let the younger generation go uninformed about the theater we knew. To the degree that I can accomplish this, through my classes and through this short book, I will carry out that promise. I would like this book to inspire the young to dare to dream and to understand the tremendous dedication, hard and frustrating work and, most important, the love necessary to come close to achieving that dream. But the effort is worth undertaking. I would like the older generation to be warmed by remembrance. As one of that generation, I remember the shy, insecure young boy who dared to dream that there was a place for him in the wonderful world of theater. How that boy matured along with his dream, and how he learned the "road less traveled" toward achieving the dream, is this book.

The mentors who inspire you and leave their passionate convictions embedded in your soul are more important than all the factual information you will ever acquire. Harold Clurman, Mark Van Doren, Robert Edmond Jones, Milton Smith and Eugene O'Neill were some of those who changed my life by giving direction to my dream and inspiring me with the true function of the art of theater.

I must tell you the miracle that God performed for me. It was very close to the end of World War II. I was stationed in London. My best friend had been seriously dating an English girl whose sister had just returned from serving the British Army in Washington, D.C., as a British Intelligence Officer. My friend was asked to find a date for this girl's sister. I reluctantly agreed to this "blind date." I fell passionately in love with this girl, Suzanne Bowkett, on our first date. I proposed marriage, but it took me three weeks of intense, constant pursuit before she gave in and agreed. Imagine: I was a PFC (Private, First Class) and Sue was a Warrant Officer. Her father was a major in the British Army, who didn't care much for the Irish, and I was a struggling actor who had one year of college, with loving parents but little prospects and no money. Suzanne became my partner and was my constant support as well as the stabilizing influence in my life. Our marriage lasted 57 years before God took her. I never could have kept on the right road without her, so I must add to my list of passionate mentors Sue, whose love was embedded in my soul--Suzanne Bowkett Fallon.

Those of the older generation may charge me with "name dropping," while the younger generation, sadly, may not know the names I drop. The important thing is to let the younger generation know that an ordinary, but sincere and passionate, young man met the extraordinary artists who helped him toward his dream.

one

"It is too bad that Dick has such a bad case of acne that marks his face so terribly. He could have been a rather good looking boy."

As I returned home from my first year in junior high school, I heard a neighbor and friend of my mother say this to her. I was not shaving yet and paid little attention to my appearance. However, after I heard this, I bounded upstairs and looked in the mirror. To my horror, my face looked even worse than it probably was. This deepened my shyness and kept me away from dances and contact with girls.

None of the above is meant to indicate that I did not have a loving family. My father was one of the most amazing men I've ever known. His Irish father could not read or write and the family lived on a small farm. His father was bright, but his mother inspired my father to seek an education. Without money, my father worked his way through Clark College and Columbia Law School on a full scholarship. His mother sent what little money she could. After receiving his law degree, my father opened a private practice in New York, concentrating on corporate law. He was very successful and moved his family to a new house in White Plans, NY. This is where I entered the world in 1923.

My father introduced me to theater at a very young age. He took me to New York, where he introduced me to the Irish Abbey Theatre Company—Sara Allgood and Barry Fitzgerald in particular. This began my love of theater.

My lack of personal confidence and shyness led me to throw myself into every high school activity I could, including debate, speech, motion picture club, theater and, most important, radio drama—all of this instead of dates, dances or personal social contact with the opposite sex. I even became the school reporter for the *Reporter Dispatch* in White Plains. I was paid by the inch (not the inch I wrote but the inch they published) and received my social security card in 1938.

My interest in radio increased as I found that I had a decent speaking voice and a flair for acting. Radio meant I could act without being seen. My work in radio in high school led me to dare to approach the local radio station in White Plains (WFAS) about seeking to start a drama program. Since it would be very inexpensive—they were the only game in town for local advertisers—they tried me out for fifteen minutes. Thinking of myself as another Orson Welles (and violating a number of copyrights, I'm sure), I brought the radio club to WFAS.

Radio at the time was the main source of entertainment. It seemed every house in the nation had at least one radio. The Great Depression was at full throttle, which caused tremendous suffering for the poor as well as most of the rest of the nation. Unemployment was at an all-time high. Banks closed, wiping out savings as well as calling for full payment of loans and mortgages. There was no social security, no safety net for the people, and most devastating was that there was no insurance on savings. My father lost everything as all of his corporate clients went under, owing him as well as countless others. When Franklin Roosevelt became President, the government began to try to stop the economic bleeding. This took time and placed the government in heavy debt. It was in this setting that radio became the cheapest form of entertainment for the country. Avid listeners made "Amos and Andy" a national hit and any attraction outside the home would not run while "Amos and Andy" was on the air. In fact, radio even sent the budding motion picture industry into an eclipse.

Even before I finished high school, I made the forty-minute train ride to New York where I learned how to seek work in radio drama. It was fortunate for all the New York actors that the bulk of radio programming moved from Chicago to New York to enjoy the talent available there.

David Sarnoff, who was in charge at the time of the Radio Corporation of America, built a state-of-the-art building in New York at 6th Avenue and 50th Street to house the National Broadcasting Company. This company dominated radio as NBC and soon split into the Red network and the Blue network (which later became the American Broadcasting Company, or ABC). Sarnoff later built the Radio City Music Hall on the same street at the corner of 6th Avenue. This was a palace of a theater that was to present stage performances as well as motion pictures. It was truly state-of-the-art facility that still is unsurpassed in the nation.

Then, to supply motion picture products for his new theater, he formed a motion picture producing company in California called Radio Keith Orpheum. Keith had been a leading producer of vaudeville and the company was known as RKO pictures. Yet, Radio was the main thrust of his development.

Next, he opened motion picture theaters throughout the country, mostly known as Keith Orpheum Theatres, to show primarily the films that opened at Radio City Music Hall and that were, of course, RKO pictures. Sarnoff even tried to corner the theater market by opening the Center Theatre across the street from Radio City Music Hall, which was to produce the best stage productions. Unfortunately, this theater did not last long and soon was closed and torn down. Perhaps his failure to incorporate the name "Radio" into the theater was the cause of its demise (just a thought). All the other buildings still exist and went a long way into making New York the entertainment capital of the nation. His National Broadcasting Company building now produces television and houses a gourmet restaurant called the Rainbow Room.

All of this, plus the live theater, was flourishing so that New York's claim of being the entertainment capital of the nation was well-founded. It must be remembered that travel to California in those days was a long and expensive train trip, which discouraged actors from making the journey to

Hollywood unless a studio had summoned them at its expense, after an audition and film test at the Long Island film studios. Film talent scouts covered the New York theater scene looking for prospective movie actors.

Going to the theater in those days was not too expensive. I got a seat in the second balcony of the Belasco Theatre for fifty cents. You could get into a movie theater in your hometown (not Broadway) for twenty-five cents. New York built mammoth motion picture palaces that featured top stage and radio performers with the big bands of the day. These top attractions would appear between the showings of the film, which meant they did five or six performances a day. These movie palaces included the Paramount Theatre (showing Paramount pictures), the Capital Theatre (showing MGM pictures) and the Roxy Theatre (showing 20th Century Fox films). It wasn't long before an antitrust suit brought by the studios that did not have a palace forced the studios to divest themselves of their theaters. Still, New York in the '30s and '40s was an exciting city offering great opportunities to actors.

It was to this kind of New York that I came before and after high school to try to prove that I could make a living as a radio actor in the 1930s. Radio at the time was all live and it was necessary to repeat programs three hours later, in many cases, for the West Coast. The sponsored programs were produced by the advertising agency that had the sponsor's account. All the major advertising agencies had large radio departments with producers and sometimes directors on the staff, who in turn would hire writers and actors for the radio shows of their clients. It is important to know that in those days a single sponsor paid for an entire program so that its product would be identified with the program. This meant that all radio actors had to audition for each of the leading advertising agencies and then follow up almost daily to keep their names before them. The agencies didn't care what you looked like but, instead, how well you could sight-read as well as your vocal range, flexibility and mastery of microphone technique. Those lucky enough to be selected for "running parts" of leading roles would be signed for thirteen- or even thirty-eight-week contracts. Anyone with a "running part" would have to sign an exclusive contract with a commensurate, negotiable salary. If you were hired for a single episode only, the pay was fifty dollars for each twenty-five-minute program. An actor who created characters such as "Mr. District Attorney," "Ma Perkins" or "Jack Armstrong" could make a good living, as these programs ran for years. It is surprising how the voice can be remembered, and in the imagination of the listeners it becomes a person they see in their mind's eye.

You also had to audition for each radio network. Each station filled unsponsored time with programs produced by the station. In all cases, the station hoped that if the program commanded a large audience a sponsor would pick it up. These were called "sustaining programs" and the union allowed smaller salaries for these. Some of the very best radio programs were sustaining, since the cost of production for the networks was minimal. They could sell fifteen- or thirty-second commercials for these, but that would raise salaries.

So, in addition to keeping contact with all those sources of employment, you needed to buy "actors' cues," which listed all the theatrical shows' casting and noted the producers and dates. New York, at the time, was a beehive of independent producers and producing companies such as the Theatre Guild, the Playwrights Company and others. There also were producers who did plays for what was called "the subway circuit." This meant that they played off-Broadway and in the suburbs. There also were productions called the "Equity Library" series, which were allowed by the actors' union to produce plays with Equity actors for little or no pay. They were showcases that the talents involved in hoped would attract agents and producers. These began in New York libraries but soon spread out to what became the beginnings of "Off-Broadway." All of these opportunities on shows had to be followed through, although most were known as "cattle calls" because sometimes hundreds of actors would show up, sometimes only to learn that the director was looking for a specific type for which the actor would not be right. The most common phrase actors heard on their rounds was "No casting today."

Joining the actors' union in those days could be accomplished only if you were hired on an Equity contract. Since some auditions were limited to Equity members, membership became important. I soon belonged to AFRA (American Federation of Radio Actors) and Equity. If you worked in films, you had to join The Screen Actors Guild. All of these involved initiation fees and monthly dues, which could become a real burden.

You tried to get to know personally as many established artists, agents or even sponsors' representatives as possible. Having your own agent was not possible until you were working.

It was at this time that I met Eddie Dowling, who then was a leading theatrical producer, director and actor. He discovered and produced the first works of Tennessee Williams, William Saroyan and Paul Vincent Carroll. He also introduced Broadway audiences to Shakespeare with Maurice Evans in "Hamlet." He was one of the Theatre Guild's favorite directors. I auditioned for him, seeking a part in "The Iceman Cometh." He said I was too young for the part in the O'Neill play, but he took a liking to me and thought of me as the son he lost. He played an important part in my professional life. So did Helen Hayes and many other real theater artists whom I met or with whom I worked and became friends.

Radio work became more plentiful for me as the draft for World War II called men to service. I had a rather high draft number but, after repeated pleading from my parents that I get a start in college before being drafted (I am sure in their minds that was to delay my being drafted), I won a scholarship to Brown University where I entered into theater and radio and enjoyed one year of true collegiate life. After that first year, I decided I could not delay my war service any longer and enlisted in the Signal Corps of the Army. Almost before I had finished basic training, I and about fifty other privates who had foolishly volunteered that we had some college education were selected to be interviewed and examined by the FBI. Those who passed this inspection were told that we were shipping out immediately to go overseas. Thus, I joined a small special detachment sent to England to work with the British, who had broken the German top secret code (The Enigma).

After two years, I was assigned to Special Services in London, where I could continue my acting and directing at the beautiful Scala Theatre, which was taken over by the United States Government to present theater and films to the U.S. forces stationed in the London area. The company of actors and directors was made up mostly of former professional artists now in service. They were combined with British actresses who agreed to work at the Scala Theatre with the American company. I met many professional artists who became my lifelong friends.

I remember an Infantry private who was wounded while fighting on the Continent and was sent to London to be treated for his minor wounds. He came to the Scala Theatre with a play he had written in hopes of getting it presented. The private's name was Paddy Chayefsky and the play was "No T.O. for Love." I agreed to direct it and thus began a friendship with a man who wrote plays for radio, television, stage and motion pictures.

While at the Scala Theatre, I acquired a copy of a new play by Sean O'Casey entitled "Red Roses for Me." I became passionately attached to it and wanted to produce it as well as play the part of Ayamon. I read parts of it to my soon-to-be wife, Sue, and a passage from the play became my testament of love to her on every birthday, anniversary, Christmas, Easter, etc. The passage is: "You are in them all, through them all, a dearer vision, a bonnie rose delectable and red."

I contacted Mr. O'Casey and poured out my passion for his play and some of my ideas for its presentation in America when I returned. After two calls, he told me I had permission to do his work in the United States. We corresponded and, when I returned to the States, I contacted Barry Fitzgerald to see if he would play the part of Brennan of the Moor. He telegraphed back that he would.

I mentioned earlier that I was shy. Yet, when I feel passionate about something, I plunge ahead and amaze myself with my daring to knock on the door and approach anyone, no matter how powerful. I was brought down to earth on this occasion when I was summoned to the office of the agent for Sean O'Casey and Barry Fitzgerald to tell me he already had optioned the play to Theatre Inc. Fitzgerald had just won an Academy Award for "Going My Way," so the agent would never permit him to leave Hollywood to work for an unknown producer when he was "hot" now in films. "By the way," the agent asked, "where have you obtained the money to produce any play on Broadway?" The bubble burst, but it didn't stop my daring to try to reach my dream.

Incidentally, "Red Roses for Me" finally was presented on Broadway in a terrible production that almost broke my heart. It closed after a short run. I received a letter from Sean O'Casey telling me how sorry he was that I didn't produce the work because my "passionate understanding of the poetic beauty of the work means so much to me." He said I had his permission to stage the play when I could and where I could.

Upon returning to the States after the war, I found that a new medium, television, was becoming more than a novelty. CBS had set up rather crude studios in Grand Central Station in New York and NBC had turned over a small part of its facilities to television. At the time, all the studios sent camera crews to cover all the games and activities at Madison Square Garden in New York. All the unions had prohibited their members from working for television because of low pay and long hours. Even so, within a few years, as technical advances were made and television sets became more affordable, TV sets started to appear in more and more homes. As the networks turned to live drama, my union became the American Federation of Television and Radio Artists and pay scales and working conditions were worked out.

So radio drama was still going strong when I began in 1946. I made my usual rounds and found some work; being a veteran gave me an advantage. I didn't try for television as it was more financially beneficial to get radio and stage work than the then lower-paid and more time-consuming television. My friends were leaving for Hollywood as they felt TV eventually would move there and film work also was possible. It meant moving to the West Coast as a base. I was married and living with my parents until we could find a place to live. I had the great advantage of living in White Plains, where it meant I was "45 minutes from Broadway," with minimal expenses. My dear wife, Sue, took a job and it looked as though I couldn't afford or benefit from moving to Hollywood. So, with the slowly changing job market in New York, I and many others were forced to examine our career paths. New York and the actors' hopes for a livelihood there would be changing forever. The number of theater productions originating in New York declined as Off-Broadway, with its lower salaries and shorter runs, grew.

Radio was fading and television soon would find that Hollywood offered the greatest pool of talent and would begin its move west. Some change and alteration of my dream lay ahead. What I had learned from my beginning was that caring about other people and trying to assist them, as well as having sincere passion, were the "road less traveled" and led to lasting friendships that became part of my passionate love of theater. The full realization of that love lay ahead.

two

Despite all of the impending changes that were taking place and that were going to take place in New York, I continued to pursue my career in radio drama. In fact, since I had become a little more successful, I began to work in evening radio. My work was on half-hour shows like "Mr. District Attorney" and a number of other dramas that were then on the networks. This paid more and it seemed as though some of the agents were remembering me, which was helpful.

Eventually, I succeeded in getting into a Broadway play. It was a play by Sidney Kingsley, who had won the Pulitzer Prize for "Dead End." The name of this piece was "The World We Make" and it was very idealistic. I played the part of a very young, aspiring man who thought he was going to remake the world. Obviously, the character eventually discovered that this was not possible. In any case, I thought I really had arrived when I made it onto Broadway in Kingsley's play. The play was not one of his great successes and it closed within two weeks. Ironically I became great friends with Kingsley.

Here at FSU, I remembered Sidney when we were doing new plays, so I got in touch with him and asked if he had a play he would like to have done. He wrote back to me saying "yes," he had completed one, and it would be excellent if we would try it out. I went to New York with the man I had hired to teach directing, Chuck Olsen, to meet with Sidney in his studio. Sidney was a painter as well as a playwright.

His play was called "Falling Man" and it concerned an artist—a painter—who had great ambitions to create paintings of which he could be proud and which would be accepted as important works of art. Unfortunately, he couldn't sell the paintings. He was told by interested galleries that he should "go paint something people want." He resisted this until his fiancée convinced him to go commercial. So the painter decided to try putting out what he considered trash and it was immediately bought up by hungry people who wanted it on their living room walls. He made some money with this. He said, "That's it; now I am going to paint seriously." His fiancée told him, "Look, your name is now associated with what you've sold and that's what they want, so you'd better give them what they want if you want to make any money." Obviously, the story of this play is something that reflected the dilemma of all serious artists. Are you going to try doing what is beautiful and perhaps starve to death? Or are you going to supply something that some of the public is willing to buy?

Well, I thought it was a very moving play, a very apt play, if you will. I hired an Italian actor who was making a big name for himself, Tony Musanti, recommended to me by his agent, my good friend Milton Goldman in New York. I had contacted Musanti and he agreed to come over and appear as the lead. He was a fine actor and did a wonderful job in the play. Chuck also directed it and I again invited a friend, Roger Stevens, whom I had met when I was president of the American Theatre Association. Roger was, at the time, a producer of promising new plays in New York. He, of course, was also the head of the Kennedy Center in Washington. Roger came to see a performance of "Falling Man," which I will not forget because he was the only one of the producers and agents who came. He liked the play very much. He met with Sidney and me afterwards and said it was a play that should be done; it holds together; it's an old-fashioned play with a beginning, middle and end. He said, "Sidney, things have changed in New York, and you write plays with large casts and big sets that no longer are financially feasible on Broadway." If any of you have read any of Sidney's plays, you know that all of them had sizable casts. Broadway, at the time I was doing this, had reduced casts and wouldn't consider anything that went beyond a three-character play because of rising costs.

Well, Kingsley had a three-set play and in it he had extras and a cast that was quite large. It really was a terrible blow to Kingsley because he didn't know how to meet the new requirements. He knew how to write only big plays, "on a big canvas," he would say. The writers who wrote plays on big canvases were not those who could get them performed in New York, not even by men like Roger Stevens.

I kept in touch with Sidney, and when he left he said he would concentrate on his painting. I loved that man and I loved what he had done in theater. It was beautiful work—when the theater was producing big plays. He was going to concentrate on his painting because the theater had passed him by.

Unfortunately, this happened to a great many playwrights because they were writing plays either too large for the present market or they were "old fashioned." I have known many of these writers. Three who come to mind are Paddy Chayefsky, William Saroyan and Arthur Miller and, in another way, there was the abandonment of Tennessee Williams. These are writers who had great distinction; these are writers who wrote—and wrote beautifully.

There is another playwright I know who is along in years now, Robert Anderson. Robert Anderson won two Academy Awards—he wrote screen plays ("Tea and Sympathy" and "Never Sang for My Father") that are well-constructed. But this man, with Arthur Miller, became lost because the new crop of producers were searching for contemporary work stressing the new morality. Who's Robert Anderson? Now audiences don't know. He wrote plays about his family, "I Can't Hear You when the Water's Running," "Never Sang for My Father." And "Tea and Sympathy" was an extremely successful play.

I went to see Bob and he showed me a new play of his, "Free and Clear." He offered it to Florida State University grads to produce, and I wanted to do something to commemorate his great contribution to American theater. I hate to see people who have measurably added to the theater all of a sudden cast aside, forgotten. Don't forget the people who built the American theater because they prepared the way for you. I have not given up on a tribute to Robert Anderson.

I tried to do it for Sidney Kingsley. I tried to do it for Tennessee Williams. I tried to do it for William Saroyan. These were all people whom I met when they were just a little bit out of fashion. I tried to help them, and that is what I'm trying to express—my concept of how to succeed in the art of theater is to care about the people and treasure those who work and try to produce the art. Therefore, when you can, try to assist them and assure them that they are not forgotten.

I'll never forget, when I taught in Maryland, that I went to New York and ran into a man whom I had been in touch with years ago when I was working there. His name was Stark Young and he was the critic for the *New York Times*. He became the critic of *The New Republic* and he also wrote books. There is no more astute analyzer of theater than Stark Young. Young translated Russian works and many of them became the English standard translation of those authors.

When I met him, the poor man was living in this little apartment, not on the fashionable East Side, and his apartment was filled with books. I said, "Mr. Young, would you be willing to come to Baltimore to talk to my students?" He said, "yes." All of a sudden, someone took an interest in him. I told him, "I want you to pass along to my students the concepts you've espoused in your book" (which I *still* require). The book was called *The Theatre*—a very insightful work if you want to learn the craft of acting or directing.

Later on, I got a call from Young. He asked if I had any students I'd like to bring to New York. Well, I took a group up to New York and over to his apartment, and he gave every one of them copies of his translations. He was a wonderful man and a great critic. He, too, had been lost in the shuffle. I guess what I'm pointing out is that as I was doing my rounds I learned the importance of caring about the people who had done such wonderful things in the theater, and I thought I could learn from them and I also could make them realize they weren't forgotten.

Well, back to my search for work in theater or radio. One day I was making my rounds to the agents and producers, looking for work, and it started to rain. I didn't have raingear or anything. I was trying, as much as possible, to avoid getting wet. As I was going along, I saw an empty storefront. There was a sign that said 'Welcome, come in.' I thought, 'At least I can dry off.' I went in and there were some chairs and, maybe, twenty people sitting there. There were people on a platform above.

It turns out that these were some of the members of the Group Theatre. When I sat down, the first person they introduced was Harold Clurman, who was a critic for *The Nation* for a while. He was the "Messiah" of theater. He was one of the founders of the Group Theatre, a wonderful set of actors that got together to produce plays *they* thought should be produced.

I sat there and Clurman started to speak. I became mesmerized! I mean, he was better than Billy Graham. He was truly inspired, passionate and really had a concept of what the art of theater was, or should be. His favorite phrase, which never left me, was "The theater is a temple. A temple made by Man to try to reveal the beauty and wonder of Man, and through that an avenue to God." He said the theater had a function; that it was not merely entertainment; that the function of theater was to provide people who were at wit's end (the Depression was on) with an experience of beauty and confidence in themselves.

The theater gives an experience, and the experience is that of human beings performing in a world created by a playwright, closely resembling the world from which the audience comes. "Well," Clurman said, and he seemed to be looking at me at the time, "you who love the theater must drive out the moneychangers."

Yeah, I'm thinking, I'm one of those. Why am I doing this? I'm trying to make a living. I'm in this garbage. In addition to doing various soap operas and doing "Mr. District Attorney" (God, what a poorly written show), I was doing this all for money!

Yeah. It didn't make any difference to me if I had any respect for what I was doing. To give you some idea, in those days radio was live and the sponsors wanted to dramatize their products. I did many commercials for Crisco shortening. They had me sound very young, of course, and I played a young boy who is running downstairs and he sees his mother in the kitchen. And I say, "Whatcha making, mom?" And she says, "I'm baking a cake for you, son." And I reply, "Oh, that's wonderful, mom. I hope you're using Crisco." And she says, "I would never use anything else, son." Well, those are not necessarily direct quotes but they're close.

I got paid for everything I did, and as I sat there with Clurman I found myself thinking, 'What am I doing?!' I now urge all my students to ask themselves the same thing. I ask them: "What are you doing it for? Fame? Trying to make lots of money? What?" I say, "Why are you really interested in theater? Because that will determine what your career in theater will really be like."

When I heard Clurman, you might say I was born again. Not a born again Christian, but I understood what I wanted to achieve in theater. I went up to Clurman (even though he could be very sharp with you) and I told him: "You just opened my eyes. What in the world can I do?" He said, "Just try to be part of those who want to produce the theater that I'm talking about." And I said, "Oh, the Group Theatre." And he said, "Yes, that's one." "But," he said, "none of us earns our living by performing in the Group Theatre. That isn't why we're here. We're here because we want to do something important in the theater, and then we have to make a living somehow, selling encyclopedias, waiting tables, doing something, doing whatever you have to do. But don't mix up the two."

This was so ironic. I heard this and I said, "I guess that's the truth." How was I, as a very minor-league actor, going to influence what is produced? I was not a star and couldn't choose material to be produced.

I'm jumping ahead a little, but I wanted to tell you the irony of this. Many years later in Tallahassee, I invited another great director whom I had met, José Quintero, to come to FSU. Quintero was one of the founders of what was called "Circle in the Square," which was way down in an old abandoned factory or something in Greenwich Village. This was a group of actors and directors dedicated to the art of theater and Quintero was one of them.

He came to Florida State to talk to the students, which I wanted him to do. He said he was given a copy of Eugene O'Neill's "The Iceman Cometh." José said, "I was transfixed." He told himself, 'I have to direct this play. I have to.' At that time, O'Neill was dead, so Quintero had to go to Carlotta, O'Neill's widow, to get permission to do "The Iceman."

Well, it already had been done by a good friend of mine many years prior and it was not successful. In any case, Quintero got permission and he chose one of the actors who was part of the company, Jason Robards. Jason took on the part of Hicky and it, of course, became the definitive production of "The Iceman."

Quintero told the FSU students this: He would never direct a play he did not find interesting. One of the students raised his hand and asked Quintero if he ever directed things he wasn't inspired to do. Quintero said, "No!" The student said, "How do you make a living?"

Quintero said, "Let me clear up something. These are two different things. Sometimes they go together, but this is rare." He said, "What you need to do is never prostitute the theater to make a living. No one working with me at Circle in the Square could make a living, but we could make theater of which we were proud. Out of that theater came some fine actors and actresses who went on to be very famous and, more importantly, to be very great artists in the theater."

What started for me as a statement from a wonderful man who touched my soul deeply continued in a man whom I admired greatly who tried to touch the young people at FSU with the same message.

After I had heard from Clurman (I kept in touch with him and I met through him any number of fine people, wonderful people), I knew something had to change. I didn't want to go back to the moneychangers and, yet, I wanted to make a living—I had to make a living. At that time I was married. What was I to do?

I went back home to White Plains to talk to my lovely wife, Sue, and my parents. I told them of my experience and said I didn't know what I was going to do. I loved the theater but I wasn't strong enough yet to know if I could influence it, and I didn't know if I could even join the Group Theatre.

My father suggested that I speak to Milton Smith, a classmate of his in college. Milton at that time was head of the theater program at Columbia University in New York. He was a character like none other I'd met. Milton was the only person I'd ever met who could have a cigarette hanging out of the side of his mouth and talk to you at the same time, while never moving the cigarette. He had this gruff way of talking. He said, "I'm glad you met Clurman and he inspired you, as well he should. I was in the professional theater." Milton turned me on, too. He turned my urges into something more tangible. He said, "Something needs to be done."

The colleges and universities turned their backs on the profession of theater. They thought it was too commercial. They spoke against the profession. Yet they were training students who wanted to join the profession. At the same time, the professionals would never, ever hire a college graduate. They thought the students' heads were filled with all types of junk. The universities of this country had made a home for writers, composers, poets, sculptors, musicians, but *not one* had made a home for playwrights, actors and theater people of any kind. By the academic, the theater was not considered an academic subject.

Milton said I could change that, if I would get my degree and go out and become the missionary to change the situation. Now *that* would be fulfilling what Clurman said.

Well, he touched me. I went home and told my wife, "I'm sorry. You thought I was going to be the great Laurence Olivier, but now I realize I am in the wrong end of the profession. I will never be a star." I thought my influence on theater would be negligible. I had one year of college and I wanted to go back and get my degrees because I had a mission that came right out of Clurman and Smith. I wanted to apply to Columbia. She said, "Go. Do it. It's what you want."

I was lucky at that time, being a veteran, that there was the GI Bill, which gave veterans funds to pursue education. So I filled out the application and was accepted to Columbia. This began my journey in another direction toward my dream.

I should point out that the GI Bill was extremely helpful in making the college degrees possible. Despite the timely financial aid, it was necessary for my wife to work full time as a secretary. I had to take a job on Saturdays at the McBurny YMCA in New York taking care of children whom I took on trips and amusing them all day. Perhaps this is why I am not as fond of children as I once was. In any case, I'm trying to point out that working to try to support your college work in theater, or whatever, has been and still is necessary.

Working in the summers as a Good Humor man and selling encyclopedias door to door were among a great many jobs I held. Although Schrafts restaurant is no longer in New York, it was at one time *the* first-class restaurant on Broadway. Schrafts had the best ice cream and was a place where well-to-do people went for lunch and supper. If you went in, you would find that every waiter was a struggling actor. Schrafts' management would hire actors and the actors would make up the schedules they wanted to keep. Even those actors who were doing programs on radio knew the hours they would be needed. It was one of the places budding actors went to earn an income, which was badly needed.

After I had received my bachelor's degree and had left Columbia, I immediately looked for work. At that particular time, colleges both large and small were finding unlimited numbers of students and, therefore, all of them were looking for additional professors and teachers to meet those demands. So, even with my bachelor's degree (and I might add that I started looking for a job as soon as I received it) I had two offers: one was from Bates College in Maine and the other was from a small Lutheran college in upstate New York called Hartwick, in Oneonta, up in the Catskill Mountains. Well, Bates wanted me to teach debate while Hartwick wanted me to teach theater. Obviously I took the Hartwick job. And it so happened that my wife had just given birth to our daughter and had just gotten out of the hospital, making it even more urgent that I find steady employment. I don't remember exactly, but I think the salary at that time was $1,700. I bought a small, old car with a rumble seat and my wife and I, with our infant daughter, traveled up the mountains to Hartwick.

At the time I was there, the college had an enrollment of about 400 students, which had expanded from about 200 based on the enrollment of veterans. I will never forget it. In my first class at Hartwick in 1948, I had a number of fine actors and actresses. I had, for example, Howard Millman, who later applied for work with me and whom I hired to be manager of the Asolo Theatre in Sarasota. To this day, he is producing director there. Also in my class was a boy named Tony Trissolini, a fine actor and young man who went on to become dean of Ohio U's theater program. We had a number of others who went on to careers. It's amazing to me that there were so many who seemed to have so much talent.

True to my discussion with Milton Smith, I immediately decided that even Hartwick should have a relationship with a professional theater, which showed something of my innocence. I formed a company called the "Leather Stocking Players." We found a place and converted it into a passable theater in the autumn. The professional group was made up mostly of students and some members of the community. We did not go to the professional community in New York because we were operating on a shoestring. But I did pay the actors in the company so you could, technically, call them professional. I remained at Hartwick College for four years and in that time I obtained my master's degree and was starting work toward my doctorate. Since I had my master's, I felt I could move up, and I did.

It turned out that there was an offer in Baltimore to be an assistant professor at the University of Maryland-Towson, in a suburb of Baltimore. So I moved my wife and children (we had another child, a boy, born in Oneonta) and we moved to Towson where there was a large student body. They must have had 6,000 students at the time and there was an established group of students very interested in theater. I named them "The Sock and Buskin Society." I decided this school should have a professional company and I found a true friend out in Baltimore who helped me form one. This didn't last too long because there was a competing professional company and we were much like the little company formed in Oneonta in Hartwick.

But I did move again, after about three-and-a-half years at Towson, and I made a grave mistake. A friend of mine, whom I knew from Hartwick, had moved to Jacksonville, Florida, and was part of Jacksonville Community College. It was a small college started in Jacksonville before a state university was established there. My friend told me about a beautiful theater in Jacksonville that was looking for someone to be the producing director. I thought, 'Well, here's my chance to be a director.' My friend said that if I took the job he would be happy to coordinate with me educationally. I looked at the job but I didn't look too closely. I was warned by people from UM not to go. They said I had a future in Maryland and that I shouldn't go to Jacksonville. My wife wasn't as sure as I, and she was absolutely right.

three

We went to the Little Theatre in Jacksonville, which still is a very beautiful community theater. I discovered upon my arrival that this theater had gone through a traumatic experience. They had fired the former producing director. A very wealthy man named Carl Swisher, who owned the Swisher Cigar Factory, headed the board of this theater and he hated the former producing director. Well, the former producing director opened a theater in Riverside, a suburb of Jacksonville, and took with him a great number of the community actors. It was a sad situation of families broken up, and they were more concerned about making this new theater fail than seeing their own succeed. The most ridiculous thing I was told to do was to take an option on every play on Broadway. This was the kind of pettiness that went on.

I could see this was not the place for me because it was being run as a revenge theater, without any thought of the product—theater. I wanted to leave at the end of one year, but they asked me not to. So I stayed there in Jacksonville for two years. But I had learned something: The community theater was not a place for me. I'm sure there are many fine community theaters, but the artistic control you have is very limited because they will have a committee of the board that will select the plays and approve the casting, so you have to be very political to survive. This bothered me a great deal because it took away the authority of the director. I mention this because you need to be cautious in taking a job in community theater without careful, full exploration of the job and theater.

At the end of two years, I left Jacksonville. I received offers from upstate New York and then I got an interesting call from Dr. Clarence Edney, who at the time was head of the

Department of Speech at FSU. He said there was an opening in his department for someone to teach speech and theater, and he invited me to come over and see him. I said to my wife, "Well, it's only a short distance away. I don't think that's where I'd like to be, but I don't want to jump into those other places."

So I went over to Tallahassee from Jacksonville and interviewed with Edney. In those days, the university had heads of departments. Then, the head was appointed by the dean of the college, not elected by the faculty, and had strong authority over what happened in that department.

Edney was a man who had very definite ideas as to what he wanted. He didn't want the speech department, which consisted of speech, speech correction, argumentation and debate, TV, theatre, and oral interpretation, to have one part dominant over any other part. So theater was one of the parts he wanted to be no bigger than debate or TV, speech, etc. And you couldn't take theater too far without running into Edney's philosophy. He offered me the job and I took it, and we moved to Tallahassee.

I discovered soon that Tallahassee was not exactly a culturally thriving city. I guess the reason I began to think of it in terms of staying more than one year is that a new university president arrived at the same time I arrived. He was hired from the University of Chicago and he brought with him some very young and very, very dynamic young men whom he wanted to head the graduate programs. He wanted to loosen up what was going on at FSU. These men came from a northern school, which was far more sophisticated than FSU (which was the Florida College for Women until '49, when a lot of faculty was brought in and it was made co-ed). FSU did what a lot of colleges did. It expanded to take advantage of the growing veteran population.

In any case, I saw something I would recommend highly to you as you evaluate a college position. The change of administration and the fact that the school was young made it desperate to grow and become a major university, equal to the

University of Florida, the main university in the state. At that time, there were only three state universities: UF, FSU and Florida A&M University, which was begun because of segregation. There were no minority students at FSU or the University of Florida.

What did impress me, though, was that this was a young college looking for what might place it in the upper ranks. What could they do in their position of youth to compete with bigger, more established universities? Whatever it was, they wanted to do it as quickly as possible and strike out with a mission of their own. That impressed me. These men were open to almost any creative idea that would advance the school to a position of at least state recognition. Therefore, I found I could do things in developing theater that I could not have done in more established universities.

If you go into college teaching, you should carefully examine the prospects. The big universities up north and out west are well-established and they have very strong tenured faculty. I think you all know what tenure means. The faculty member has been there for some time and the faculty member is assured a lifetime position, unless something very serious happens. The tenured faculty members can be or become rather conservative and set in their ways. Any young person coming in has to contend with such faculty members who may not want, as my father used to say, "the dust moved off the desk." In other words, they don't want to create anything new—they just want to stay as they are.

Don't look at salary as the inducement. Look at what chance you, a faculty member going in at a lower rank, will have to commit yourself to develop a program in theater that will allow you to have some degree of creativity and expression. Therefore, I would choose a smaller university or college that is in the process of trying to establish itself. Then, if the administration is creative, they will look at anyone with a smart idea and say, "Let's see if we can't do something."

It was in that atmosphere that I talked to the new dean of the College of Arts and Sciences, and I said, "I want to see theater developed. I would like to develop the union of the profession of theater with the educational theater. And, therefore, I'd like the concentration of *this* theater to be on striking out to do something that Harvard, Yale, Columbia, etc., aren't doing—putting the focus on, and concentrating on, performance. Let theater history and the more academic areas be covered by the mainstream universities with their big-name faculty that we can't bring here. That's not to say we wouldn't do theater history, but it wouldn't be the dominant force."

This sounded different to them. In fact, we would be pioneering something that would be developing in the universities around the country—and we could be first, perhaps. Maybe we can do it in a way that immediately will create excitement. They said, "Do what you think will advance the theater." This was from the dean. I asked, "Would you be willing to let me have a little money? Would you be willing to let me bring in professionals—right away? I would like to start by introducing new works that are being 'tried out' for potential commercial use." "Oh, yeah!" they replied.

I immediately went back to my New York base and got in touch with Eddie Dowling. Eddie, who produced the first plays of Tennessee Williams and William Saroyan, was in the process of producing work as well as he could, but the theater in New York was diminishing and becoming more difficult. Since I had met him and had become a friend, I presented him with an idea: "Why don't we establish this tryout of new plays at FSU. You would become the producer, along with Florida State." That sort of struck a note with him and he came.

This was almost my second year, making it all somewhat precarious. Eddie announced he had raised $12,000 and had a new play that he would like to try out at FSU. He said he would like to bring in three professionals to join the university company. The set and costumes would be created by the university and we would have a run of one week and see how it went. Well, Eddie arrived in Tallahassee.

I explain this only to show you how different things are now. No one had ever given the university $12,000. The FSU Foundation was in its infancy. The idea of universities seeking private funding was relatively new and certainly FSU had not yet gained a donor base.

When Eddie arrived, a big story was published in the *Tallahassee Democrat* that Eddie Dowling, distinguished producer-guild director of Eugene O'Neill, has come to Tallahassee with $12,000 to produce a new play in conjunction with the university theater and he brought with him three professional actors. I can't tell you what kind of vibes that set off, not only in Tallahassee, but it also reverberated around the state. The *St. Pete Times* and the Jacksonville paper picked up the story. Even Gainesville, home of UF, reported the story. UF did not even have a theater at that time. They were performing in a high school auditorium and they, too, had neglected theater, thinking that was secondary to the speech department. We were lucky at FSU because, if UF had a thriving theater, they would never have let us in the door because UF had the political clout. Most of the members of the legislature were grads of UF, so you had to tread carefully because they were very careful about which programs they would allow FSU to develop.

When we announced this, Governor Farris Bryant asked to meet Mr. Dowling. So we went in to have an audience with the governor, who acknowledged the generous gift Eddie was making.

In any case, we began with a play called "Assignment in Judea," written by Patrick Walsh, who lived in Palm Beach, Florida.

We had the three actors Eddie had brought from New York. I can only say that the theater really can excite regular people—some of whom are very poorly schooled in theater but who go to the movies. They are very, very interested in show business and the famous people they've seen who had come in, and they will fawn over them.

At the same time, we were in the capital city with the legislature, so we could court legislators who were impressed by the fact that I was starting to bring in big-name people. Let me illustrate what I'm talking about.

Eddie brought in the female lead in this play, a motion picture actress during the '40s and '50s. She was what you might call one of the glamour girls who was employed in a lot of "B" pictures and minor roles in "A" pictures. Her name was Louise Albritton. Well, that name doesn't excite most of you who are reading this. But, at that time, most people had seen her films, and they were going to show one at the local motion picture house. Louise was the wife of a very famous commentator on TV and radio, and she was our name star.

Eddie also brought in an actor named Khigh Dheigh, who looked Oriental. At that time, "The Manchurian Candidate" came out, which Frank Sinatra helped to produce. It was taken off the market because it was a story of the indoctrination of a son by his mother (played by Angela Lansbury, who later made her fortune with "Murder She Wrote"). She got her son brainwashed by the communist cause and used him to infiltrate them. Sinatra played one of the officials and Khigh was the villain. "The Manchurian Candidate" was reissued and is now considered a classic. The movie had just come out and Khigh wore a mustache like Fu Man Chu and had a bald head and slanting eyes. He was famous because he had made a film of recent vintage.

The third actor, Fred Tozzere, was a noted Broadway actor but not a film actor. So that was the professional cast, along with Eddie.

I started something in a little theater that was not really designed to be a theater—called the Conradi Theatre at the time. It had big windows at the side, which made it impossible to get a complete blackout, and a small stage that wasn't very deep. Space was very limited and there was no wing space and limited fly space. Everyone had to dress downstairs and come up an iron staircase to make entrances. So this stage had certain limitations that made it not exactly an ideal theater. We had torn drapes that you could pull across the windows. The theater did not have air conditioning at the time (though they were beginning to air condition everywhere else).

This was the place in which we debuted the Eddie Dowling/FSU New Play Series. In this very little space, there was one other faculty member besides myself there to teach theater and speech. We all taught 18 hours of speech and theater and did theater work. That was quite a load, and we also had to do advising. We had one technical director, Charlie Reimer, who built the sets, and we had a lady who did the costuming. She wasn't actually a costumer, but she was a woman from the department who was willing to make the costumes. That was our department and our facility that greeted these people from New York. They obviously had some trepidations, but they had worked in worse theaters—Summer Stock and other dinner theaters—where the space was quite limited.

Anyway, I want to express that this was an amazing idea and, although we didn't have nearly the staff, facilities or students, it created such a stir that photographers and TV's one channel in town, Channel 6, were there. Everyone took an interest and we got publicity from all sources. This was the talk of the university and the state. All of a sudden, FSU had something that could cause a stir, and this is what I had hoped would happen.

While doing the Dowling New Play project, I decided with Eddie to produce Mark Van Doren's play, "The Last Days of Lincoln." As I began preparations, I received a call from Eddie telling me that Julie Haydon, who had been married to noted theater critic George Jean Nathan, and who played Laura in "The Glass Menagerie," was in dire straits. Her husband, who was more of a father to her, had died, and Eddie said Julie just sat in their apartment in New York and never left. Friends brought her food, but now the rent was coming due. Some who came to see her walked off with Nathan's materials and effects. No one knew where her money had gone. In any case, she was to be evicted. Eddie said we must do something for her. I offered to have her come to Tallahassee to play in Mark Van Doren's play. I sent Eddie a ticket for her and he persuaded her to come.

Julie arrived in Tallahassee in the winter with just the clothes on her back. My wife, Sue, and I met her at the plane and escorted her to a motel room that I had booked. She kept her hand over her face while we drove her to the motel and appeared to be the living image of Laura in "Glass Menagerie". It was remarkable. She locked herself in her room and wouldn't come out. We left soup and food for her outside her door. It took quite a while before my wife could get her to come out of her room. Sue took Julie downtown and bought her an overcoat and other necessary clothes. Mark Van Doren heard of her actions and, naturally, was worried about her ability to appear in his play. Remarkably, when Julie went on stage, she came alive and did a beautiful job of acting. She called me "Saint Richard" and tried to refuse money.

My problem was what to do with Julie after the run of "The Last Days of Lincoln." She had no home to go back to and was, like Laura, completely unable to fend for herself. Mark Van Doren, who joined me in my concern for her future, suggested that he had another play, "Never, Never Ask his Name," which we could do next. This play had a part for Julie if I could raise the money. With my wife's help, we begged and borrowed enough to pay Julie and keep Mark and the play together. Julie again did a remarkable job. She remained just as shy and lost off stage as before. My problem came up again at the close of this production.

Julie was a devout Catholic, so I called a friend, Sister Marie Carol, who taught at Barry College in Miami, for help. We agreed that we would both try to book Julie at every college and junior college in the state if I could find a student to write a one-woman show for her based on her roles in "Menagerie," "Time of Your Life" and "Shadow and Substance."

I found a student who wrote Julie a fine one-woman show. He also agreed to accompany her on the tour if I could get him released from his studies to do so. The tour worked as the Sister and I pressured schools to engage her. We even did her publicity. She did the tour and accumulated a reasonable sum of money.

Sister Marie Carol found a small Catholic college in the West that agreed to hire Julie. Julie spent the last years of her life in the friendly Catholic school, which admired her so much.

Julie, like Laura, was lost without guidance. We in the theater must never neglect nor forget the fine artists who are lost and forgotten in the modern theater. They are treasures to be kept so the young can learn their craft and art.

four

This is the story of the formation of the Asolo State Theater in Sarasota. In 1959, I was directing a play in Tallahassee called "The Country Girl," by Clifford Odets. It featured some of our graduate students who would play important parts later on in the Asolo State Theater. Primarily, these were Howard Millman, Eberle Thomas and Isa Thomas. The art department at Florida State University had been conducting workshops at the Ringling Museum in Sarasota dealing with the masterly artworks that were exhibited there. The art department invited the theater department to present a play in a theater that was attached to the Ringling Museums. We accepted and moved our production of "The Country Girl" to Sarasota and the Ringling Museums. There we discovered a real gem. That was the Asolo Theater, which had been brought over to the United States from Asolo, Italy, piece by piece—including the design of the theater itself.

This jewel of a theater was the only existing theater of the 17th and 18th Century. It was the home theater for Eleanora Duse. It was where Robert Browning composed some of his poetry. It had been in the hill town of Asolo, which became quite an artistic community. As times changed, the government decided to replace this old theater with a modern motion picture theater. The old theater was taken down with the interior saved piece by piece, along with the dimensions and design, in the hopes of perhaps selling it for its historical value. It was then placed in a curio shop in Milan, Italy.

After John Ringling left his estate in Sarasota (including all of his artwork and the museum itself) to the State of Florida. "Chick" Austin was appointed as first director of what was then the only artistic entity owned by the state. By lucky circumstance, Austin was traveling in Italy and happened to see the remains of the Asolo exhibited and available for purchase. He was so attracted to it that, without any authority from the state, he purchased it for the Ringling Museum. The exact price is unknown, but it was extremely low compared to today's market. He had it shipped back to Sarasota and exhibited the interior parts of the Asolo in one of the galleries of the museum. His heart was set on reproducing the actual theater because he had all of its dimensions.

The state legislature at that time met only every other year. The legislators appropriated money for the Ringling Museums to build an office for the director. Up until that time, Austin had his little office in the museum library. What he did was to take the money that had been appropriated and build the theater on the back of the Ringling Museums. (Things in Florida at that time were not as monitored as perhaps they are today.) This went on while the state paid the bills, not knowing what was being paid for. The theater was erected and Chick Austin, who was a great fan of the theater, had what he considered to be the "crown jewel" of his Ringling Museums. Well, when the legislature discovered what he had done, they passed a bill declaring that the director of the Ringling Museums would never have an office. Indeed, there was no office for the director of the Ringling Museums until the 1960s-70s when there was a small office built.

Therefore, this is what we saw when we came with the company of "The Country Girl" to perform in this theater. The museums, unfortunately, did not quite know how to use this theater. It was opened with great flair and a story in *Life* magazine as they presented an Italian opera in the theater. Then, after this opera and the big ceremony of the grand opening of the theater, it was never occupied by live theater. They began to show motion pictures in the theater and it was part of the tour of the museum. People would go through the museum to look at the artwork, and then they were ushered through this beautiful 17th Century theater.

So we moved in and presented a performance of "The Country Girl." Arthur Dorlog, who worked with me in the Department of Speech, and Charles Reimer, who was the technical director, and I were all struck by the theater's beauty and the fact that it was not being used. We approached the director of Ringling Museums, Kenneth Donahue, and asked if he thought there would be a possibility of presenting plays there during the summer. Well, Kenny was rather taken with the theater and said it might be a good idea, but it would have to be approved by the board of directors of the Ringling Museums, which was appointed by the governor of the state. Also, it would have to be approved by Florida State University, but, more importantly, by the Board of Regents, which had control of the state universities at that time. Since they were separate state entities, the agreement would have to state which entity would be fiscally responsible for the production of those plays and how they would divide the cost and whatever profit was realized from the plays themselves. At the time (and really up to this present moment), there was great difficulty in getting separate agencies to work together in any kind of harmony because they all protected their turf. So I thought the only way to deal with this was to see the governor directly before we presented it to the university or the Ringling boards.

The governor at that time was LeRoy Collins, who was perhaps the greatest governor Florida has ever had. He got Florida through the whole integration conflict without a great deal of violent unrest. At the time, I was president of the Florida Theater Conference.

I went up to see the governor in Tallahassee and told him what we wanted to do. I said, "The difficulty is that the entities are all separate: one is the Board of Regents and one is the board you appoint." He said, "I think perhaps the best way to handle this is I shall make a governor's decree and I shall decree that Florida State University and the Ringling Museums, under the board of trustees, shall present a series of plays during the summer in the Asolo Theater." Then he said the entities would work out the specifics but each would share the cost and responsibilities for this series of summer plays. Well, when this governor's decree was presented to the Board of Regents (which, of course, the governor appointed at that time) and to the board of the Ringling Museums (which the governor also appointed), obviously both boards decided, "Yes, if that's what the governor wants, we'll do it." The Board of Regents notified Florida State University, under the governor's decree, that they would present a series of plays at the Asolo Theater. The arrangements were to be worked out between the two entities. Thus began a series of plays at the Asolo Theater in Sarasota.

Five plays that were done the first year, for 25 performances. The plays were constructed in Tallahassee by Reimer. They were cast in Tallahassee, made up primarily of students, but we realized we perhaps were going to have to go beyond our own students. So we announced that we were going to do these plays, and we enticed back some graduates. Indeed, we mounted the five plays and presented them in Tallahassee so that we could try them out. Then we had to obtain trucks and vans to transport everyone and everything—scenery, costumes, actors, directors and technical people—down to Sarasota to present the plays. The Ringling and the Asolo did not have any facilities for set construction, storage, building costumes or any facilities at all except the theater itself and one dressing room. That was the extent of the facility at that time. So we had to find a place to store all of the scenery (some of it could be on the stage).

After that first year in which Arthur Dorlog directed the plays (he was our theater historian), we were going to do 17th and 18th century comedies in the summer. Fortunately, the theater was the only facility in the Ringling Museum that was air-conditioned. During the first year, we would have audiences of 20-25 people, and the people of Sarasota sort of smiled and said we never would have people in Sarasota in the summer who would leave the beaches and attend 17th and

18th Century plays. Also, the Asolo was located in the rear of the museum, so it did not have a marquee. If we said we were going to be presenting something at the Asolo Theater, there would be many people who would ask, "Where is the Asolo Theater?" So we had a lot of things going against us.

I guess my dream, or vision, was to make a professional company of this, and to really try to use this as what Milton Smith implanted in my brain: the means of combining the university and professional theater by having and supporting a regional theater. That was the vision.

So, the second year we tried again. After the second year, Art Dorlog was completely exhausted and fed up with the attempts, so I had to direct the series of plays from that point on. Eberle Thomas (who was in "The Country Girl," you may remember) and another graduate of FSU, Robert Strane, assumed the positions of joint artistic directors. With their help, we selected plays. And I began to say, "I think we've got to break away from exclusively 17th and 18th century plays, because that does limit tremendously the appeal for the audience, and we can't afford the kind of slim attendance we are having." So we included Shakespeare, we included Shaw, we included Moliere, we included a lot of those . . . and then we began to sneak in some more contemporary work. Slowly, we began to develop a following—a group of patrons, as it were, who thought this was a wonderful thing.

In 1964, helped by a friend in the legislature, I went to the legislature and asked to get a bill through that would name the Asolo Theater the "State Theater of Florida." In the back of my mind was the hope that if they did this I could then go back and request funds to support the State Theater. Well, there was no problem getting this through because the legislature didn't think there was any money attached. And so we became the State Theater of Florida.

I wrote a proposal to the Health Education Welfare Department concerning what I called an "enrichment program" for the public schools of Florida. It would be composed of presenting plays at the schools, having the teachers include the plays in their curriculums, and having the students read the drama and then attend the play. I did get a grant at that time from the federal government to do this enrichment (around $320,000, which was a lot of money). I got in league with the County of Sarasota to help. We assembled all of the language arts instructors throughout the schools at a state meeting. Our goal was to enlist the support of these people for the program and then have them go to the principals and superintendents in the various counties to get their support for the program. The program would not involve any cost for the schools, but teachers would agree to include this in their programs. Long story short: we did get the approval of all concerned, and we started our tour of the schools.

We concentrated on the middle schools and high schools. We selected a play, cast it and had one of our people direct. Then, Brad Wallace, a very wonderful member of our company (who is still there), devised a program where he would entertainingly introduce the students to the art of theater. He would demonstrate how to watch an actor work and how the actor communicated, as well as how the designers communicated in the sets and the costumes. So the students got an experience of how to attend a theatrical work. This was a marvelous program to introduce hundreds of young people in high schools and middle schools around the state to theater.

We did this for two years. When the grant ran out at the end of two years, I didn't know what to do. But something unusual happened. We had been so popular that the newspapers throughout the state decided they would sponsor the performances in counties in which they published. By this kind of subscription, we were able to continue it for a couple more years.

It did put the Asolo Company, the State Theater of Florida, in a position where it was known throughout the state by virtue of the school tours. When the grants ran out I called the dean of Arts and Sciences, and I called the chairman of the speech department in which I was then working, and told them we had great success with these tours and I thought we had best go year-round. To do that, we would have to find a costume shop, a scene shop and we would have to employ people year-round. This would be a substantial outlay of money because it would then mean, instead of performing the plays in Tallahassee and shipping them in, we would produce them in Sarasota and present them there first.

It was a miracle, I guess, when on the phone the dean of Arts and Sciences said, "Sure, go ahead." Then he said, "By the way, how are we going to finance this?" I told him I had put in a grant to the Rockefeller Foundation, which had given money to the arts and theater. Well, that sounded good to him. In fact, we had gone through the first phase of the grant and had passed. I thought for sure we were going to get this money. Then I was called to New York to the Rockefeller Foundation.

I might add that, at that time, the first Republican Governor elected in Florida in the twentieth century was in office. Claude Kirk was a very theatrical governor. He came into office with a mystery woman, whom he would not identify, but who probably was going to be his wife. He had his own idea of saving money and made budget cuts without ever thinking of what he was cutting. One of the things he cut was a Rockefeller Grant that had been issued to Daytona Beach to support symphony concerts there. The Rockefeller Grant required matching funds and the state had signed on to provide the funds. However, Kirk cut the state fund, so the match was never made.

When they called me in they asked, "Are you with the State Theater of Florida?"

And, proudly, I said, "Yes; yes we are."

"Do you know what your governor has done?"

"No."

"Well, he has cut money from a matching grant we had made to Florida, which the governor had signed. And he has been in the press because the schools of Florida have been put on sanctions because of cuts he has made."

Kirk was rather notorious. They told me they were sorry, but as long as the theater was a State Theater they would make no further grants to the State of Florida, leaving me with about a $200,000 debt to be paid.

Obviously, it was a serious situation and being in debt up to $200,000 could not be readily overlooked. The chancellor of the university system at the time called me and the president of the university into his office to find out what in the world had happened. I explained what had happened. I guess the president of the university was a little embarrassed because not only was this debt incurred, but there also were no records in the university budget concerning the Asolo Company in Sarasota. The chancellor was interested in how this happened because the money spent was never approved in any budget he or the Board of Regents had seen.

Well, the president, as it turned out, found out that they had been taking the money (including the $200,000) from the "Coke Fund." These are funds that are taken from drink machines or from things students buy. All the income goes to the president and he doesn't have to account for it. In other words, he doesn't have to include it with the state money. Well, using this Coke Fund money obviously didn't please the chancellor. The chancellor said, "I want you to know that from now on neither Florida State University nor the State of Florida can be financially responsible for the activities of the Asolo Theater in Sarasota. If it is an educational activity, then that's different, but not if it is for support of the theater program itself. I'm going to ask the university to make up the $200,000 from the Coke Fund. You all could have been charged with misappropriation of funds, but I will not pursue this."

When everyone was chastised accordingly, I went up to see Dr. Robert Mautz, who was then chancellor, and he put his hand on my shoulder and said, "You've got a wonderful program down there, and I hope you can continue it, but you do understand that we cannot continue to be liable for what might turn out to be a deficit. So I hope you can find another way to finance it."

I want to point out to young people that we conducted this statewide program in the schools and received national publicity and a grant. If there were not such a positive reaction to the work that was being done, I'm sure my fate would have been much worse. But, frankly, the Asolo was looked upon at that time as one of the jewels in the crown of Florida State University. This was in the days before Bobby Bowden, when the football program dominated.

What I want to pass along is that the best thing you can do when you start a theater program is to put everything you can—national attention, statewide awareness—into doing the finest work you can because, if the rocky roads come, and they will, your reputation will help you even when it looks as though things are going to turn terribly against you.

Interestingly enough, I went back to Sarasota where we decided, without consulting the university, that we would have the company enter into Equity contracts—the unions. Perhaps this would help us obtain even better talent, Equity members, who would then work with us, and our auditioning process in New York would be even more successful. I had signed Equity contracts with a number of our company to begin the new season. But with this news, I had to change everything because the university and state could not be responsible. I could not sign the contracts as the head of the Department of Theater. Fortunately, I had a good lawyer in Sarasota who said we could apply for 501c3 status and we could form a not-for-profit corporation, calling it the Asolo State Theater, Incorporated. He then proceeded to do this.

The next job was to recruit local people for the board of this corporation. Obviously it wasn't easy because we had incurred the $200,000 debt, which had been written up in the papers, etc. Therefore many business people were reluctant to become members of a board that would have fiscal responsibility for the theater. Yet, with the help of some wonderful people, we managed to recruit a board. This board had me, as executive director of the program, sign contracts on behalf of the Asolo State Theater, Inc., which is in existence to this very day. That meant the theater was now an entity that was NOT accountable to Florida State University anymore. I had, however, transferred the MFA acting program to Sarasota because we had a professional company there, and it became a conservatory. The faculty in Sarasota could be paid by Florida State University. We began a dual program: the theater itself run by Asolo, and the Conservatory of Training, where the students were enrolled in an MFA program run by FSU and located in Sarasota. They never touched campus and they had their own graduation. Later on, we became a School of Theater and I was made its dean. We eventually were admitted to the National Association of Schools of Theater (NAST), which meant any student coming out would be accepted because it was accredited by NAST.

One of the things NAST required was that the MFA in Sarasota become a three-year program, compared to the MFA on the main campus, which is only two years. In Sarasota, students spent one year as members of the professional company. The conservatory took off and became extremely well-received. In fact, for three years the program was rated among the top five in the country by *World News and Report* in its annual review of universities. Recently, it was named by the *New York Times* as one of the top nine.

My dream and objective, which was to unite the universities with the professional theater so we would become related to the profession, resulted in the students having a link with the profession, thus making them more easily accepted in the profession.

This came a lot easier because regional theaters began to crop up around the country. Theaters that had been in existence as touring houses did not have much to choose from because the stars on Broadway refused to tour anymore, which dried up the professional theater for the various regions of the country. To take the place of the professional touring companies from New York, regional professional theaters developed, hiring Equity actors and really doing some nice work. The Asolo Theatre became one of these regional theaters, and I, along with three others, formed what we called the University Resident Theater Association (URTA). We tried to get universities interested in having professional companies so their students would have the same advantage and could join the URTA.

URTA set up auditions in three parts of the country—New York, Chicago and Washington—to let students audition. URTA developed and there are now about 60 members; it has become the dominant element for students who want to enter the profession. The advantage to the students in the academic world is that now they do not need to go to New York or Los Angeles to find work. There are, for example, more Equity contracts in Florida than in New York City.

One of the other things that developed at the Asolo was a format for other regional theaters in the state. The University of Florida formed a professional company in Gainesville.

The Coconut Grove Playhouse in Miami was up for sale by a producer in New York because the touring program was so weak. He did not produce anything onsite—he just brought in companies. He sold the Coconut Grove to the State of Florida for a bargain price. The state then accepted a company that existed in Miami to appear as a not-for-profit company at the Coconut Grove Playhouse. Regional theaters began in Boca Raton and soon in almost every major part of the state.

I decided, since we had the "State Theater" name, I would try to pursue funds from the state legislature. By diligent lobbying, I did get some funds from the State of Florida. Unfortunately, our base in Tallahassee was not the most powerful part of the State of Florida because the population in South Florida had more representatives and senators who were interested in their own regions. So I decided to expand. After a good deal of negotiations, we had the Coconut Grove, the theater at Boca Raton and the theater at Gainesville named state theaters and we then had a group of state theaters.

I went to the Secretary of State's office which, at that time, controlled the funds for the distribution of money for the arts—the Cultural Affairs Division. I said, "Now that we are a state organization, we should be under your jurisdiction, and I would like to submit an annual budget to be included in your budget." Well, he agreed, so we had a separate item— State Theaters of Florida—and we requested funds from the legislature. Since the legislators were supporting their own areas, we did pretty well.

This is an important thing to think about if you are in any way trying to form a theater company professionally, even if it is affiliated in some way with a university: Try to tie it in to the state.

Just two years ago, I visited a graduate of the Florida State University School of Theater who runs a theater program in Abbeville, SC, and who was struggling. I told him to make the Abbeville Playhouse the State Theater of South Carolina. I helped him write the request in legislative form, and last year it was named the South Carolina State Theater. I said, "Now, you can go in and request money for the state program because they should be obligated to pay for something they created."

There is no question that the money that has been appropriated by the NEA, the government and locally has been declining each year. Therefore, you have to think of other ways to get funding; and what I have been through is one of the ways. I would caution all of you that it's very difficult to start something. But the dangers that come after you succeed also can be very important.

Once you have done something that seems to work, there are many people who will want to take it over because it's already a working proposition. I have had to fend off two approaches, one by the University of South Florida in Tampa and then, recently, the administration of Florida State University, which wanted to bring the program back to

Tallahassee to save money. A battle ensued and I came out charging. We won that battle.

It is important to make friends with the legislature, particularly in the area where you exist. When FSU tried to move the program back to Tallahassee, I learned the chairman of the senate appropriations committee was from Sarasota and had a vested interest there. The Asolo board made it quite clear: Don't come back unless the Asolo stays where it is. Well, since this senator was chairman, she could use a little arm twisting. If the university pursued this course, it might lose some of its appropriations. This helped and brought about reconsideration, and the university dropped the idea.

All of this is just a precaution: If you start something and it works, there always are going to be people who want to take it over. If it's of value to you, then it's of value to them. I think this will be the conclusion of the Asolo program here and what I wanted to do. Even though the theater was not supported by Florida State University anymore, by putting the Conservatory in it, it became the laboratory for students who were attending. Thus it is an important aspect of FSU training.

I cannot overstate the importance of obtaining as much publicity as you can—hopefully favorable—to cement the program in the minds of a university administration. What I did was look around, and I discovered the theater critic for *The Saturday Review of Literature*, Henry Hewes, had been a classmate of mine from Columbia. Henry was wonderful. He came four times to Sarasota and wrote glowing reviews. His first one was to congratulate Florida State University on establishing something so essential in regional theater. This was the first national article written about Florida State University at that time. When that got to the administration, they were very impressed.

I then got in touch with Norman Nadel, who at that time was with the *New York World-Telegram* and *The Sun*. He came, thought the program was wonderful and wrote a stunning article in the New York paper. Eventually, we were reviewed by *Time* magazine. I cannot tell you how much this meant to the administration, which depended upon the reputation of the university to get funds from supporters and alumni. This did a tremendous amount of good because these people knew nothing of theater. Eventually they came, once we got national attention, to see what was going on. But they would not have taken any notice if it had it not appeared in the national press that something good was happening.

I add this: I was terribly fortunate that this occurred in 1960 before Florida State University had a football program that gained national attention. We were the first element of the university to gain national recognition.

While working at the Asolo Theater in Sarasota, I had the good fortune to meet Audrey Wood, who was one of the most successful and famous agents for playwrights in New York. She had moved with her husband, William Liebling, to Sarasota because of her husband's ill health. I think she had made the decision that she would retire from her position in New York in order to care for her husband in a better setting for his illness. I met her at the theater and she invited me to their home on Long Boat Key. I got to meet Mr. Liebling, who had been the agent representing Marlon Brando as well as many other famous actors.

Audrey said she would be happy to do something to help me. She suggested that she might give a playwright's workshop. She would select the writers she felt showed great promise. Each of these writers would be brought to Sarasota and she would work with them on the development of their work. Then, when she would come to the decision that the work had reached a successful point, the Asolo could produce it, the playwright could see it performed and she would try to bring in agents to see it. This sounded great because, up to that point, nothing like this had been done by a regional theater.

When Audrey announced that she was going to do this, we had the attention of all the press in New York and everywhere else because of her distinction in her field. Then she chose three writers to come to Sarasota and worked with them for the better part of a year as they worked on their scripts. Finally, she selected the writer she thought was ready and we produced his work.

Meanwhile, her husband, Bill, pleaded with me to see if I could arrange for an honorary doctorate for Audrey. He felt she deserved it since she had introduced so many great writers to the American theater. So I got back to Tallahassee and submitted her name. Yes, eventually it passed. Not only the University committee, but also the Board of Regents approved the awarding of the honorary degree.

Audrey continued with her workshop until her husband, Bill, passed away. On his passing, I think she felt she would return to her profession in New York and give up her Sarasota residence. I told her what I had done and said I was terribly upset that her husband did not live to see the awarding of the degree. I did tell him that I had submitted it and it had been approved. It turned out that everything was set up to be done at the opening of the Fine Arts Theater. So it was announced and invitations were sent to some of the writers whom she had developed.

five

My next project was to find a suitable opening for the theater, which I thought should be some kind of a celebration of what we had accomplished, and what we were hoping to continue to accomplish. Audrey came to Tallahassee and, when she arrived, she was written up in the papers. A man named Chandler Cowles, who had a horse farm outside of Tallahassee, read about Audrey and came to see me. I introduced him to Audrey and told him she was going to be here talking to our students (at that time I had established a playwriting program in theater).

Chandler had dabbled in theater himself. He produced "Billy Budd" on Broadway and had produced the operas of Gian-Carlo Menotti. In addition, he helped raise money for Menotti's Festival of Two Worlds in Spoleto, Italy. He, Audrey and I sat down. Audrey, of course, knew Menotti and had represented him in this country. So they both agreed it would be wonderful to get Menotti here. Chandler said Menotti had just finished his first play. Menotti was determined to write a non-operatic piece because his operas were noted for their melodramatic and theatrical flare.

Chandler and Audrey both got in touch with Menotti over in Italy. Yes, Menotti wrote back, he would be happy to have his first play, "The Leper," produced for the opening of the new theater in the Fine Arts Building at Florida State. I said, "That's wonderful!" Except that I had to go and try to find some money to bring him in. Audrey was very helpful in that respect because she was awaiting her degree.

Menotti arrived. He had his script and he wanted to hire two professional actors to come in to appear in his play. The rest would be students. Well, the next thing that happened was that Audrey and Chandler got together with Menotti and said something to the effect that, "You have a tremendous following of very wealthy people and artists from every facet of the art world who come to Spoleto, who are very, very interested in anything you do. Wouldn't it be a great idea to invite all of these people to come to see your first play!"

Menotti said, "That would be just wonderful!" He said he had an assistant back in New York who would make out the invitations and send them out. I thought this sounded exciting.

A series of meetings started, which I shall never forget because Audrey got into it as well and started inviting her New York acquaintances. We received notice from New York that Greta Garbo had accepted, and William Schirmer of the Schirmer music publication firm had accepted. They came in droves, names like . . . well, everyone from the pretender of the Italian throne to the Italian ambassador. They were starting to say they were all interested in coming.

Then Audrey and Chandler told me, "You'd better do something because you can't expect these people to come individually; it's got to be done in some good way." Chandler said we should charter a plane that would come from New York directly to Tallahassee, because there was no direct service at that time. We'd fly them in from LaGuardia to Tallahassee and bring the whole group in at once. Wouldn't that be something! Charter a plane? I will never forget this . . . speaking of risks. I went to see the university president, Stanley Marshall, who kids me about this to this day. There had been news almost constantly, not only locally but also in New York papers, inquiring as to how this was proceeding. It was something that even had international implications because of Menotti's reputation in Europe. I told him that Menotti had all these friends and some of them were coming and that we'd even gotten word that Greta Garbo was coming. I said that Chandler and Audrey felt we had to charter a plan to bring in these people and that it could be the biggest thing Tallahassee had ever witnessed at one time. So he agreed. He said he would get in touch with Eastern Airlines to charter a plane and proceeded to do so.

I, meanwhile, realized I had put my foot in it because Marshall said, "Now this means there have to be ninety people coming because, if that plane arrives and only about six people get off, you and I are in deep trouble." He smiled and said, "Well I'm telling you, you will be the one in the worst trouble, okay?" I said, "Yeah, I know."

I proceeded to try to keep one foot in Sarasota and one foot in Tallahassee. I used Audrey to go back and forth while she was waiting, since she had not returned to her New York office. I was on my way with Audrey to fly to Sarasota when I got paged at the airport. It was Marshall on the telephone. He said, "Dick, I wanted to let you know that tomorrow is the last day I can cancel that chartered plane without having to pay for it. So tell me, how many actually have accepted?" I said I'd get right back to him. I called Chandler and asked how many definite invitations had been accepted at that point.

He said, "Oh, now, old boy, don't worry about it."

I said, "Tomorrow is the deadline for canceling the flight and I'll be out of here if it turns into being a . . . . How many? How many Chandler?"

He said they had six definite.

I said, "Six?!"

He said, "Well, that's definite. There are a lot more coming."

I turned to Audrey and said, "Oh, my God, I don't know what to do. Six!"

She said, "I know I've got a lot of people who will be coming, too. But you know these people wait until the last minute to accept these invitations."

So, I called up Marshall and said, "Don't worry, the plane will be filled."

"It will?"

"Yes."

I proceeded on to Sarasota and said, "Audrey, please get in touch with someone. My God, we've got to have that plane filled."

Meanwhile, the head of the FSU Foundation decided that he would go on this plane and meet the celebrities in New York to make sure everyone (the crowds of people) got on. In those days, I might add, we had no such thing as cell phones so you had to get to a telephone somewhere, and they did not have telephones at that time on airplanes.

Audrey was to receive her honorary doctorate. We already had people flying in on their own, critics from New York. The critic from the *New York Times* arrived to review the play. Chandler had invited a lot of friends. Two people had arrived, but not from the plane.

I said, "Chandler, do you have any idea?"

He said, "No, I've lost communication. The assistant has given up now and said he's going to LaGuardia to make sure they get on." The assistant did not tell Chandler how many people were boarding.

Meanwhile, Marshall, who anticipated all these great people coming in, had arranged to have a big luncheon for them all. Marshall had asked me, "How are we going to house all these people? They'll have to be taken care of while they're here."

Here's where my wife was very important. I decided that I would, with her help, round up the most noteworthy citizens of Tallahassee (noteworthy meaning moneyed) and invite them to become patrons by paying $100 each for the privilege of meeting these celebrities at the airport and taking care of their housing and food while they were here. Wouldn't that be great? With the help of my wife and Mart Hill, Louis Hill's wife, we rounded up sixty or seventy to help. Of course they were all wondering whom they would be meeting and who the big celebrities were who were coming. I told them it was a big secret. I was figuring out how I was going to get out and find another job.

We sat at this table waiting for the arrival of the plane. Stanley kept asking, "Have you heard how many are on board?"

I said, "No, and the president of the Foundation hasn't checked in; he never called so we don't know. The plane has left La Guardia. We know that because the assistant to Menotti was there."

"Didn't he tell you how many?"

"No, he had nothing to do with counting them as they got on."

We sat there, and here were all the patrons who had paid $100 sitting at the luncheon, and the president and even the head of the Board of Regents were there. This was the biggest anticipated event. Audrey was there, of course, because she was to receive her honorary doctorate that afternoon. Eventually, someone said the plane had arrived. I sat there and in they came. I am telling you—Tallahassee has never seen the like.

There was everybody who was anybody in society, both in Europe and in this country. Yes, the pretender to the throne was there, the ambassador to Italy, Tony Randall and every big star, including Helen Hayes. It was the biggest assortment of poets, musicians, composers, dilettantes, politicians, everybody. Ninety people came. They were all jolly because the bar had been open on the plane, so they had a great time. They arrived and everybody was excited seeing who was there. I thought to myself, 'Thank God!' Tony Randall acted as the Master of Ceremonies and said, "We're happy to be here; we're looking forward to this." He turned to Audrey and kissed her and said, "I also understand we're celebrating your doctorate!"

It's a wonder I didn't have a heart attack. It turned out to be the biggest event the university has ever staged, then or now, because there were 90 very distinguished people in every area of the arts. I told Mart to be careful when assigning the patrons because they'd all want to go with Tony Randall or Helen Hayes. I said to tell them everyone is important. Some of them had to take two of the celebrities.

The patrons were just gushing over this and they became friends of the theater. Lou Hill went out and played golf with some of them, Some others took them out to introduce them to Tallahassee while waiting for the premiere. It was a great success after having been a great gamble.

Audrey went through the honorary degree ceremony. And the astounding thing was that this was all before the premiere of the play. Menotti was busy because he was directing his work.

All of a sudden, Tennessee Williams entered the back door with about four distinguished playwrights. Luckily enough, Tennessee Williams had just been released from a rehabilitation center where he had faced his addiction with drugs or alcohol. He was in good health, which was not always the case. He was in excellent shape and hospitable. I took it as my responsibility to entertain Audrey and Williams.

It was interesting because I not only took Williams to the play that evening, but he also stayed the next day. Williams talked about his plays and said what he liked and what he didn't. He gave me a recording of his whole experience with "The Glass Menagerie" and Eddie Dowling. And he told me about how he was so upset with the way "A Streetcar Named Desire" had been performed. It was directed by Elia Kazan, who directed "On the Waterfront" and, of course, was very well known. Kazan decided he was gong to hire Marlon Brando to play the part of Kowalski. Williams was terribly upset because Kazan allowed Brando to just take off with the part. The result was that Brando, more or less, took over the play even though they had a wonderful cast in the play in New York.

Anyway, he was about to go and try to stop Kazan and reprimand Brando but he decided to call Audrey about it. Audrey said, "Look, you're getting the production by a noted director. It's going to be a hit. Now, if you start messing with it . . . . Brando's a very temperamental actor. Don't start telling him what to do . . . ." She said, "Don't you need the money, and don't you want to have the production go on?" Then he went into what he really wanted to do with the play. As you and most people probably know, Tennessee Williams' plays were almost always centered on the female. He wrote wonderful parts for women, for actresses. This, again, was the case in "Streetcar," and it was not to be centered on Kowalski. Blanche was the central character and she got lost in the shuffle. Williams told me how he would like the production done. I was determined to do the play the way he wanted it. I was terribly impressed because Williams was such a sensitive man. Obviously, you can detect that if you read his work.

Williams left me with an incomplete or unfinished play. Unfinished meant he never had done rewrites on it. He said, "You can have this," and I still have it. Williams spoke to the students and he attended the premiere. As I've mentioned, he spent the next day here, as did the other visitors. It was the most astounding two days in which there were more distinguished people visiting the campus than I can ever remember.

It all started with the idea of bringing in someone who had his own following—Gian-Carlo Menotti. And, of course, there was Audrey Wood, who also was very distinguished in the professional theater. We had never been reviewed in the *New York Times*, and here was "The Leper," Menotti's work, reviewed in the *New York Times* as having premiered at Florida State University. I can't tell you how much that meant. I think the reviews, as well as the common sentiment, were that the play would make a very wonderful opera. Menotti obviously was disappointed but, much later, he turned it into an opera.

I guess the reason for relating all of this is that I took a very big gamble that could have turned against me. If this plane had arrived with very few people and, if those who were there were of little distinction, my gamble would have ruined me. However, gambles that are carefully examined are necessary in this business. It was something the patrons talked about for years afterward.

Another person who came was Milton Goldman, one of the most distinguished theatrical agents, who belonged to the same agency as Audrey Wood. Milton represented probably the most successful actors in New York and even in Hollywood. He was one of the most giving individuals. Milton lived with his friend Arnold Weissberger, an attorney. They had a wonderful, large apartment overlooking the East River. I and my dear wife, Sue, were invited to all kinds of parties because Milton was so taken by attending this premiere with all those celebrities. He thought it was the greatest thing since cream cheese and that, since I had arranged all this, I obviously was famous. He wanted me to visit him every time I came to New York, and I did. Then, when I arrived, he would say: "I'm giving a party tonight; I want you to come." I remember one party Sue and I attended at his apartment. It was filled with lots of people—Hermoine Gingold, Carol Channing and many others.

So Milton came and introduced me to everybody as "the great producer of the most exciting premiere he had ever attended." Then he said, "I want you to meet this man who just arrived from England. I think Audrey's going to represent him when she comes back to New York. He was quite a success in London." That was Andrew Lloyd Webber, who had just arrived because his production of "Cats" was about to open. Milton became the best friend I ever had in New York. All of a sudden I was famous, at least in the eyes of Milton Goldman.

Once I started this patron group and they had met all of these famous people and paid $100 for the privilege, I tried to get them to continue their support of the theater. My wife really got started and developed the Patron Association, which still exists in the School of Theater. The problem was that they would all come to me and say: "Who are you inviting in next?" They were so intrigued by these famous people that they became patrons—not for the students, which was what I wanted, but to meet famous people.

I called Milton and said, "Milton, I have a little problem. I have to keep these patrons happy because they're going to support our program, and they all want to meet celebrities." Milton said, "Fine, I'll send someone." It began like this, and then Milton would send in his clients. The people he sent in were all known television, film and Broadway stars; every month there would be someone coming in. This always would occur at the time I was asking for money from the patrons, of course.

One of the celebrities who came to us from Milton was Maureen O'Sullivan. For those of you who aren't old enough to remember, she was Jane in the original Tarzan movies. But, more importantly, she was the mother of Mia Farrow, who, at the time, was having an affair with Frank Sinatra. It was all over the papers. Mia Farrow was a very attractive girl and Maureen O'Sullivan was very famous in her own time.

Anyway, I had a reception for Maureen O'Sullivan. Unbeknown to me, she had gone to the president of the university, who at that time was Bernie Sliger, and said she had left her wallet at home and wondered if Bernie could lend her $100. Bernie didn't think too much of that but he gave her the $100. Maureen was very popular and sweet. I had arranged for the theaters to show an old Tarzan film. Bernie came up to me and said, "I loaned Mrs. O'Sullivan $100. Do you think I'll ever get that back?" And I said, "Oh, Bernie. I wish you had told me." I mean, I'm not talking against her, but actors are phenomenal in the sense that they've always forgotten something and they want to borrow money. I don't know, but the percentage of returns is not great, so I said: "Oh, my Lord." Well, believe it or not, she did return the $100 with a nice note and her daughter, Mia Farrow, signed it, too. That is kind of sideline information about the sorts of problems I had with having these people come in.

Carol Channing was a very petite, ditzy woman but very popular, not only because of "Dolly," but also because of "Gentlemen Prefer Blondes." The funny part was that she had in her purse all of these fake diamonds. Even though "Dolly" was terribly successful, "Gentleman Prefer Blondes" was perhaps her most famous role. So she would go up to a man and drop a diamond in the man's hand. These are the kinds of things that went on as a result of the opening of the Fine Arts Building.

I became so friendly with Helen Hayes that I had another fortunate thing happen. I had met her earlier in New York when she was doing a play for which I had auditioned. As you might know, Helen's husband, Charles MacArthur, wrote "Front Page" with Ben Hecht, and a number of other very popular comedies. She was very concerned that he had died without getting enough attention for his playwriting.

One of our graduate students, who was doing a thesis on Charles MacArthur, was told he might find materials in the Ohio State University library. He went there and he found among all the boxes a play by MacArthur. It had never been seen and I thought, as did Helen, that it had been lost. We produced this play and Helen was ever so grateful. She brought in her brother-in-law, John D. MacArthur, who was at that time one of the richest men in the country. I found out what she needed most, which was to get a little more attention for her husband. So I convinced the MacArthur Foundation to print the complete works of Charles MacArthur, including this new play entitled "Stag at Bay." This was another way I had of cementing a relationship with this wonderful, famous lady.

Helen began to make films for Walt Disney. Some of them were pretty good. Some of them weren't. One she made was called "One of our Dinosaurs is Missing," which was going to be distributed by Walt Disney. She convinced Disney to have the premiere in Tallahassee, Florida, and she would come and Disney would send his Disney characters here: Mickey Mouse, Donald Duck, etc. She arrived with the Mickey Mouse characters and the mayor and the governor had arranged for her to ride in an open limousine. The Disney characters led a parade down Monroe Street.

The premiere was held at the old Florida Theater, which doesn't exist anymore. It was the biggest of the theaters in town.

"One of our Dinosaurs is Missing" was a typical Disney film and we filled the theater. There was press present since Disney wanted to make a big deal of it to promote the film. Helen gave the money received for the showing to the university's School of Theater.

Helen was so helpful to me that we started something called the Charles MacArthur Center for American Theater. We started collecting some of the best materials in American theater. We had this so-called "center" located in what is now the Radisson Hotel. Helen said it would be wonderful if we could develop some videotapes of some of the great Americana plays that were lost. She wanted to start that series with a play called "End of Summer." We obtained the rights and she played the lead. We filmed it down in Sarasota. Channel 13 in New York showed it twice on Masterpiece Theatre on PBS. Helen was a tremendous help to me and the university and to the School of Theater in particular. All of this came out of her feeling that the School of Theater was doing something to advance her husband's work and giving recognition to him as a playwright.

I visited Helen at her home in Nyack, NY, where she had left intact everything that was her husband's. She was an extremely lovely lady and a fine actress. She was proud of only one film.—"Airport." This was the film that won her an ___ ved to show it to budding actors because ___ le of acting. Maybe that's the only good ___ treasure it for that.

six

Due to many friendships I made over the years, some of which I already have mentioned to you, I was fortunate to learn a great deal about some of the major happenings and developments in the American theater. One of these was getting an unusual, if not unique, insight into the eventual production of "The Glass Menagerie" in New York. Not only was this play one of the most moving experiences in New York theater, but it also firmly established Tennessee Williams as a major American dramatist.

Audrey Wood was the agent for Tennessee Williams. She saw in Tennessee's early one-act plays that he had a great gift for writing poetic drama that reached into the very soul of his characters. Audrey wanted him to write a full-length play (which would be much easier to sell to a producer) for a possible New York production.

Tennessee came to Audrey with a one-act play called "The Gentleman Caller," which she thought showed great potential for developing into a full-length play. She had Tennessee add to his existing one-act play an outline of what might be a full-length version of the work. She sent this material to Eddie Dowling, who you will recall was an independent producer in New York and who had done some very fine work in introducing writers to American audiences. Eddie was so taken with what existed, as well as what was outlined, that he took an option on the play.

It was at this point that Eddie started meeting with Tennessee to flesh out and develop a full-length play. It is hard to say what Eddie contributed toward this development of the play and what Tennessee did. But neither one would deny that the other had made a very important contribution toward what became "The Glass Menagerie." Eddie suggested the title after the development of the first part of the play, which gave an insight into the character of Laura and her separate world that existed primarily with her glass figures. It also was a title that seemed to encompass more than just the appearance of the gentleman caller and indeed gave Laura a full-blown character, which would be the driving force of the play.

When the work seemed to be complete, Eddie began trying to raise money for production. He was partly successful in raising the necessary funds, but he needed something that would be a catalyst for attracting greater attention to the work. Remember, Tennessee Williams was then unknown; this was his first introduction to Broadway. And Julie Haydon, who was to play Laura, had been successful in a number of plays but was not the kind of star who could attract big money. Eddie did something that all of the "old-timers" on Broadway thought to be a very serious and "wrong move to make." He called upon the actress Laurette Taylor.

Laurette had been a very successful actress and was considered to be, in her time, one of the great actresses. Yet she had not appeared on stages in New York in recent years because she was an alcoholic. Producers, therefore, feared engaging her for performances because she could not be depended upon to stay sober. Eddie felt she would be ideal to play the mother in "The Glass Menagerie." So, when he went to see her, he took along a copy of the script. Even without further investigation, he offered her the part of Laura's mother, Amanda, in his Broadway production. Laurette was afraid and very skeptical about accepting such a large part because she knew her own weaknesses. Even if she made commitments and promised to stay sober, she knew she was not strong enough to follow through. She told this to Eddie. Eddie thought about this but felt it was worth the risk if he could get the performance from her that he felt she was capable of giving. So he reiterated his offer. She finally accepted and completed the cast.

When it was announced that Laurette Taylor would be appearing in the lead in this new play by a new writer named Tennessee Williams, a great deal of press occurred. It was mainly critical press, which went into all the stories of Laurette's behavior in past productions and why she had more or less been kept from appearing on Broadway. Eddie found that the interest in seeing what happened did attract a great many people to the play, but it did not do a great deal to raise money because people were fearful she would not be able to deliver.

Eddie scratched together enough money to begin rehearsals and he decided to try the play out in Chicago. Eddie and the company went there during the worst blizzard that Chicago had experienced in many years. The opening night, in fact, was at the height of the blizzard, so the audience stayed away in droves because they either couldn't get to the theater or they were afraid of being stranded at the theater with the snowstorm raging.

Fortunately, Claudia Cassidy, who was the leading drama critic for the *Chicago Tribune*, did attend the opening along with the very small audience. This small audience discouraged the backers, who knew they had to take in enough money not only to pay for the expenses of the Chicago production but also to give them a possible head start on the New York productions. Everyone was discouraged, and Tennessee Williams was ready to give up because this seemed to be a sign that Broadway was not yet ready for him.

The next day in the *Chicago Tribune* appeared one of the finest reviews that Claudia ever wrote. She raved about the play, the performances of the entire cast and, in particular, the performance of Laurette. This, as they say in the business, was a "money review," meaning that that kind of review, sent to New York, would encourage advance sales of the play when it was due to come there. Audiences did slowly pick up as the storm abated but, no doubt about it, the two-week run lost money for the backers. This meant they had little money left to bring it into New York.

There was great discussion, and a number of those backers pulled out and said they would not contribute any more money because they didn't feel they could make their money back on such a production.

An interesting footnote was added by Julie Haydon. Before the opening, she and Eddie were walking along a street in Chicago and went by the windows of the biggest department store in Chicago, Marshall Fields, which I believe still is in Chicago. Eddie looked in the window and stopped, and Julie said, "That is exactly the dress that Laura would wear." And Eddie said, "Oh, yes!" He did not have the budget to hire a professional costumer and had to buy costumes for his cast so they had picked up what they could from Goodwill stores, and so forth. Julie felt that wearing that dress would give her a very good feeling for the character of Laura.

Well, Eddie walked into the department store and asked how much that dress would cost. It was quite expensive, at least from Eddie's standpoint, and it was more than he could afford at that point. So he asked to see the manager and the manager came. He introduced himself and he introduced Julie and he told the manager that she was going to star in this new play that was going to open up in a few days called "The Glass Menagerie." He said the dress in the window was exactly the costume needed for the character, Laura, to wear. He asked if there was any way, outside of buying it, to use that dress in the play if they returned it. The manager said that this store was a very upscale store. They did not rent out their clothing because they could not, in good faith, sell a used piece of clothing to a Marshall Fields customer who would have to pay the full cost. "But," he said, "Would you give us credit in the program?" Eddie said, "Oh, of course. We'll give you an *ad* in the program." These plays were out-of-town tryouts and the plays that usually came to Chicago went on to New York and succeeded. "Well," he said, "we would like ads in all the programs of this play wherever it is produced professionally." Eddie said, "Yes, of course."

The manager thought about it and said, "All right, I'll write it off as advertising." Well, that was the dress that Julie wore for the tryout and, indeed, for the New York run of "Menagerie." And it was interesting when Julie mentioned this to me because, after the success of "Menagerie" in New York, along with the review by Claudia Cassidy, the play was extolled as perhaps the finest play to be developed in America that particular decade. Marshall Fields had its ad in the program, as was promised, and ended up putting a copy of the dress on a mannequin that was placed at the very front entrance of the Marshall Fields store with a sign under it that said "The Laura Dress." I am told that if you go into Marshall Fields, it is still there today. It didn't say, "The Glass Menagerie." It said "The Laura Dress," and that was enough. There weren't too many people who had anything to do with theater or who visited the theater who did not see "The Glass Menagerie."

Eddie had to scrape together enough money to put down the advance that is required to book a Broadway house. Therefore, he sent a copy of the Claudia Cassidy review to his friends, the Schuberts. He said he would like to bring the play into New York but he didn't have the wherewithal to put down the money on a commitment. Well, the Schuberts were impressed. But, let me say this: they were more interested and impressed by money than anything else. However, one of the houses had a play that closed early. Perhaps you already know this, but if you put down a sum of money to book a theater, you are given the theater for a period of time. The sum is how much money that play earns every week. So, if you read *Variety* or any of the trade papers in New York, they list the box office revenues of the plays each week. There is a clause in the contract they give to producers that says, if the box office revenue falls below a certain sum, the owners of the theater have a right to evict them. Now, that doesn't mean they will evict them, because, if they don't have a show that wants to come in, they'd rather have any production there than none at all. They get a percentage of the box office sales and want to be sure they're getting as much as they can. But if it's at the height of the season and there are plays waiting for theaters to open up, of course it's obvious that the theater will invoke that clause and evict that play in favor of a new one.

Well, they had a playhouse in New York that had evicted a play that was doing poorly. The producers had withdrawn the play because they were losing so much money. They had no play to put in then, so they said Eddie could come and occupy the theater (he didn't have to put up any money) until another show came along that would offer the advance money and be a potential moneymaker from the standpoint of its commercial value.

So he went in without any protection of having even a limited run and stayed in the situation where he could be evicted at any time, regardless of revenue, if they still wanted to move to another production. This was a very insecure situation under which they moved into this theater for "The Glass Menagerie." I can never express the kind of experience the audience had in seeing that production. Laurette Taylor was magnificent. All of the reviews were as glowing as they could be. All of them pointed out that Laurette was giving the performance of her lifetime.

Obviously the play sold out, and Tennessee tells the story of trying to get the Pulitzer Prize and Academy Award winning playwright Horton Foote into a performance. Horton accompanied Tennessee around to the stage door, and there was Eddie Dowling. Tennessee said, "Have you got a seat that I can give to Horton Foote?" Eddie said, "No, we've sold every last one. However, if he wouldn't mind standing, you can go in and stand." So Horton went in and stood because, upon seeing the play, he, too, thought it was magnificent.

As I said originally, Eddie Dowling was with me for so long that I got his story of his production of "The Glass Menagerie." And when Audrey Wood came in for her honorary doctorate, she gave me a voice recording of, as she called it, her remembrance of "The Glass Menagerie." Audrey would say that sending that play to Eddie Dowling was what she considered a last resort. But no one else would do it.

Tennessee Williams' biggest complaint against Eddie was that he made certain changes in the script. For those who read the drama, you will remember that Tennessee had put screen projections in certain places. These projections were of blue roses, and there were little sayings that seemed to be key in the scenes that would follow.

Well, when production came, Eddie cut all of those projections and all the little statements that Tennessee wanted projected on the screen before the scene began. There are those who feel that was an extremely wise move; there are very few productions I've seen that did include the projections.

Julie Haydon told me that Eddie was very kind to her. He particularly assisted her performance during the gentleman caller scene in which she was to show some reaction after learning he already had a fiancée. She said she had trouble, and it was Eddie who gave her the way to handle it. And it must have worked because it was always successful.

Eddie may have those who criticize him, mainly because he always seemed to be doing productions "from the seat of his pants." He had very little money to put into productions. He had a small group of followers who would invest mainly because they had the same principles and beliefs he had about the future of American theater, which depended on getting promising new writers produced so they could establish themselves and add luster to the American theater. I might add that this is very rare on the Broadway scene. There were those who produced new works and were interested in the same principles as Eddie but their work was done in Greenwich Village, way off Broadway. The audiences they attracted were small in comparison. Being on Broadway, even to this day, means a lot more than being produced somewhere else in New York. Everyone, every playwright, every actor, looks toward being on Broadway. That's what Eddie gave to Tennessee Williams, William Saroyan and many others.

That is why I always have revered Eddie. I try to put his name forward as the founder of the New Play Festival I started at Florida State University. And I tried to give him every credit I could because I felt he needed every bit of affirmation of his accomplishments. I owe it to the young people to help them never forget those who have made such contributions to American theater and who are not, at present, part of the mainstream anymore.

Because of age, because of the way theater has changed, the cost of the production of a Broadway show today would have prevented Eddie and his style from doing anything. Even the most economical productions on Broadway were far in excess of anything Eddie used in the production of his plays. Eddie always will be in my heart. Eddie, in my judgment, has not gotten the kind of recognition he deserves for what he has done.

One of the problems that Eddie ran into with the run of "The Glass Menagerie" in New York was that Laurette Taylor frequently would come to the theater quite drunk. They tried to sober her up with a shower and by walking her around the block. Sometimes that worked and she would become sober enough that she could go on with the performance.

By the time the show opened in New York, the press absolutely went wild with praise for Laurette. It was a performance that probably never would be repeated or excelled. She was able, despite all the problems with alcohol, to give such a stunning performance that people came just to see this actress who had been quite famous in the past come back to make, as it were, a comeback, and do something that probably was the greatest performance of her career.

So the audience members in the theater were all there to see Laurette Taylor and, if Eddie and his wife were unable to sober up Laurette sufficiently, Eddie had to go out in front of the audience to announce that Miss Taylor was indisposed and could not go on with the performance that night. Naturally, most of the audience not only sighed, but they also had the right to ask for their money back or to exchange their tickets for another date.

Well, Eddie, working on a shoestring budget, did not want the audience to ask for their money back, so he did something I had never heard of before nor since. The Equity Association requires that the leading actress and actor have an understudy. The understudy had to go to a minimum of rehearsals, come in just before the curtain was about to go up and stay for about an hour or so to make sure the actor or actress he or she was covering went on and was well. After that, the understudy was permitted to leave.

It also was a requirement that the management of the production put into the program a list of the understudies for the actors with the statement that the understudies never would appear in place of the principals unless stated before the performance.

Eddie did something that was not detected at the time. He did not list the understudy for Laurette Taylor in the program. He did that because he knew he was going to have to do something rather dramatic to prevent audiences from leaving if she did not appear.

He hired an actress who, at that time, was very well known in the motion pictures as well as on the stage. Her name was Allison Skipworth. She was a big woman and had played in many comedies and dramas and was quite like Laurette in appearance. Eddie asked her to get up on the part and then come to every performance and sit in the orchestra of the theater.

If he had to come onstage because Laurette was indisposed, he would make the curtain speech by saying to the audience: "Now, I know you've come to see Miss Taylor, and I am so sorry that she is not available to perform tonight. But, before you leave, I see someone sitting in the audience! Ladies and gentlemen, sitting in the orchestra is Allison Skipworth! Now, Miss Skipworth is a good friend of Laurette Taylor's. She was so pleased to know that Laurette had come back to Broadway. But, I'm sure that if we give her enough applause she might do the performance for us tonight." Well, by this time, the audience was applauding and she stood up and looked around as if saying, 'Well, I just don't know if I can do it on such short notice' and tried to look very hard to get. Of course, this made the audience clap even louder because they thought this was unexpected and that she just happened to be at this performance.

After a suitable amount of applause, she graciously acknowledged and said "yes," and she came up to the stage and was greeted by Eddie. Again, she bowed and they all gave her applause and she said, "In a few minutes." Of course, she had costumes backstage that were made for her and she got into them and got ready to go on since she knew the part quite well. The audience never wondered how she got that costume to fit her so well. While she was similar in build to Laurette, it would have been difficult at the last minute to get a costume belonging to someone else to fit you. So all she did was get into the costume and go on.

I don't know how much money this saved Eddie. And, in fact, he was using Allison as the understudy for Laurette, but he never acknowledged it in the program so he could do this trick of making the audience feel like: "Oh, my gosh. This is exciting. You had to be there this particular night because any other night she wouldn't be there, of course." They didn't know she was at every performance and, when the Intermission came, she would leave if Laurette could go on.

That, by far, was the cleverest ruse of which I have heard. I don't know how many times he had to do that, but it was many, I'm sure, because Laurette was slipping badly due to her alcoholism. I don't think this was ever revealed publicly, and certainly not by Eddie, so nobody ever caught on. It never occurred when the critics or press were there, so the audience assumed it was a really small miracle when she came in and could do it. I'll never forget that, and I told Eddie he was as clever as could be. He said if he hadn't done that the losses would have been considerable.

seven

I received word when I was the dean of the School of Theater that Burt Reynolds wanted to call on me. At the time, Burt Reynolds probably was the highest-paid motion picture actor and was No. 1 at the box office. We set a meeting time and he came to Tallahassee accompanied by a small contingent of bodyguards and hangers-on. Burt sat down and told me he wanted to complete his undergraduate degree at FSU.

It turned out that Burt had enrolled at FSU and was here at the university for one semester. He had come to play football and started on the team. Unfortunately, in the course of playing, he hurt his knee, which prevented him from continuing as a football player. Very disappointed, Burt left Tallahassee and went back to where he and his family had settled in Jupiter, Florida. I looked up his record and found that he had left school without ever withdrawing and therefore he received F's in all the subjects he had been taking. So he had practically no credits toward the degree he was seeking. I tried to explain to him that it would be a major job for him. Obviously, a lot of credits could be offered for his professional work but there were other stipulations that would be needed for a B.A.

This discouraged him, and he then told me he was opening a dinner theater in Jupiter. He said he would very much like to have an institute of training established with the dinner theater. This institute would be for students who had aspirations of entering the motion picture or television industry. It was primarily an institute where students would learn from him and people he would bring in about what exactly the business required in motion pictures or television. At the time, the state university system did not have a film school as such. There were some television courses offered and, obviously, there was a TV studio operated by the university, but these were taught by more academically trained people than those who had been in the profession.

So I agreed that I would at least help him start this institute. I took some time from my supervision of the Asolo to go to Jupiter and I outlined what I thought would be a legitimate program and how to recruit the students. I also suggested a person to head the program. I did not stay long at that time because, obviously, I was busy with everything else. He picked my brain, so to speak, and learned my reason for starting the Asolo and the kind of School of Theater I envisioned.

I returned to Tallahassee thinking I was finished with Burt's dinner theater. I got another call and Burt came to see me in Tallahassee again. This time he had a new plan. This plan was to build a new theater. This theater was to house professional stage productions but it would have attached to it in the rear a taping facility. Whatever was presented on the stage could just be moved back into a studio that would be almost exactly the dimensions of the stage of the theater itself. Then he thought he could tape the shows and, of course, he hoped to sell that to TV. He said he would give this theater to FSU.

I said, "Well, that's very kind and I hope you can achieve this." He said he could think of no one else in Florida who could pull this off but me and that, since I had been so successful starting the Asolo in Florida, I would have to be the one to execute his plan. I said I was very honored and pleased that he thought I could do this but I already was trying to run programs here in Tallahassee and Sarasota as well as administering the School of Theater and I really didn't have the time to do that.

It so happened that the legislature had set up a program for the state universities where they encouraged outside donors to make a contribution to a university that would be used to set up a chair occupied by a distinguished professor. This would be a $1 million chair and the universities would live on the income from the $1 million. The legislature said that if the donor would give $600,000, the state would give $400,000 to make the $1 million chair.

Obviously, the universities wanted to get in on this as quickly as they could. The University of Florida, which was the dominant university, had a number of its alumni make pledges. Some of these pledges were to be worked on for a number of years. Some would be in the wills of the men and women, so it would not accrue to the university until their deaths.

Burt had read about this and when I said I couldn't do this because I was the dean and had all this work, he said, "What if I set up a chair for the School of Theater?" Then there would be room for someone like myself to be paid a good salary and occupy the chair, which would give me the time. "Well," I said, "Burt. I don't really know. I'm sure the university would love the chair because this is something they obviously are desperately seeking."

He said he'd see me later, walked out and went to see Bernie Sliger, the president of the university. Burt made the proposition to Bernie and said he wanted to set up this chair and build and establish this theater with his concept of the videotaping facility. This would be a commercially viable arrangement and would earn money. He said I was the only one he thought could do the job.

If I agreed to serve, he then would supply the money for the chair. I, of course, did not know about this until I was called to the president's office and, in a very humble way, the president asked if I would consider this for the university— because if I retired as dean and accepted the post of the new Burt Reynolds Chair, this would mean $1 million for the university. It would mean they would perhaps own another theater, and it would be an innovative theater because it would make use of the newest elements of technology. I told him I was still working and trying to develop things here and I really didn't want to go into this tremendous job of trying to find a place and a designer for this theater. I really wasn't interested. I said that Burt Reynolds was very glib at this time and it might not even come to pass, so I might be out there looking for something that never would happen. Well, I left Bernie with that.

Apparently Reynolds kept calling Bernie so I got another call from the president. This time a member of the Board of Regents was in Bernie's office, as well as a member of the Cabinet, who happened to be an FSU alumnus. And they went over it again. They said Burt was not going to continue his offer and wanted an answer because he then would have to look elsewhere. Of course, he was threatening to withdraw the idea of helping the university.

I might add that Burt already had put hundreds of thousands, if not millions, of dollars into the university, almost exclusively into the athletic program. He bought new uniforms for the football team. The university built a dormitory that was named after him. He had been generous to the university and they, of course, wanted that to continue. His career was at the top of the box office still, so they were sure he could deliver the theater. But he wanted me because he had heard about my work at the Asolo, etc., etc.

They put pressure on me to accept his offer and, after the session, I said I'd need time. I came back and talked to my wife. Sue was not too happy about it, and obviously it meant we would have to leave Tallahassee to find a place because he wanted it to be in Palm Beach County, preferably around his home in Jupiter. Then he added to the pot, as it were, by notifying the committee that had talked to me that he'd be happy to come up to address the legislature to convince them to appropriate money for the building of this new theater. But, of course, before he would do that, he wanted to know I was in. I might add that the legislature is not immune to the influence of celebrities any more than is the general public.

The committee knew that the legislature probably would appropriate something for this purpose (money was not as tight as it is today). So this was one more thing they wanted and it was all up to me. Well, the pressure worked, and against my wife's doubts I capitulated. Oh, I was making the greatest sacrifice for the university, as the members went on and on. I retired as dean and would be appointed to this forthcoming chair. As soon as Burt heard this, a check for $600,000 arrived at the university within a matter of a week.

The university went gaga because FSU won the race. We had the first funded chair of any of the universities. The University of Florida was green with envy because it had promises and commitments, but $600,000 wasn't appearing. This was celebration time and I was looked upon as the great savior. Well, it was ridiculous.

Then Burt was all over me and wanted Sue and me to come immediately to Jupiter. When we arrived by plane we were greeted by his henchmen. Anyway, we got there and were given an antique Lincoln car. At that time, Burt had collected antique cars and he said I could use this one for my stay there. The car was a very wonderful antique, but it was antique. Anyway, he offered me an apartment to stay in in Jupiter. So we moved into the apartment and the legislature met and Burt went up and, yes, lo and behold, the legislature appropriated $3 million for this new theater that Burt Reynolds called "The Theater." This had to be given to FSU because you couldn't give it to an individual, and it made headlines all over the state at that time.

When Burt came to Tallahassee, Sue and I invited him to our home to have supper, not realizing what this would mean. He came in his limo to the Capitol, and the press was there to cover his meeting. As soon as he took off, everyone knew he wasn't going to the airport. As soon as the limo took off, all of the press came; and I don't know how many, but there were carloads of girls who followed this limo; and there was the police escort, of course, because the girls would drive up in the wrong lane just to see him and wave to him.

Well, of course, they all arrived at my home and I thought the place was on fire. The police came and the girls came in their cars and my street was full of cars, all up and down the street. The girls came out in front of the house as we were going to have this little dinner. As Burt came in, the girls started chanting "Bu-urt" and they quite obviously were settling in until he would come out and address them. He asked if they would disperse if he were to come out. The girls finally agreed to leave if he'd come closer. He talked to them and he touched some of the girls, sending them into ecstasy. The police stayed, while I thought, "Oh my, what have I gotten into here?"

We moved to Jupiter and I was besieged by real estate people and property owners wanting to supply the land for this building. I had to come back and, with the help of some of the staff of the school, like Charlie Reimer, I put together a draft for what we wanted to present to a theater architect. Burt already had approved this and it was approved by the university.

Next, we drove around and looked at the sites. The competition got so great that these people offered the land for free. And so I took Burt to see the land.

Meanwhile, the *Palm Beach Post* decided there must be something in it for Burt Reynolds and that he was pulling some kind of clever trick to get the state to build him a theater. So they started writing editorials attacking him and had cartoons lambasting him. In fact, they did a real hatchet job on Burt, who got furious and called me in. He said he was through with Palm Beach County and that we were not going to build a theater there. He would not do anything for Palm Beach. I had looked at land and worked for almost a year. Now where was I to go? It was at that time that I learned the Asolo company was to be evicted from the Asolo Theater, so I said, "What about Sarasota?" He said, "Yeah, yeah, sounds good; you set it up."

I went to Sarasota and told them Burt was interested in having the theater there. They then became interested and Burt went to talk to them, with the police escorts and the whole thing all over again, like it was the President who was coming in. He addressed them and the people were awed. "Smokey and the Bandit" had been there to sell-out crowds. He told them, yes, he'd like to pursue his dream of a theater, told them Dr. Fallon would head it said and it would be great to have a theater with the professional work and the taping facility, too. This would not have worked, of course, if the Asolo Theater could have continued, because it would have been competition for the Company. But he invited the Asolo Company to come and perform and use his theater.

I spent five years away from Tallahassee trying to bring about this new theater. The committee in Sarasota said it would raise money because Burt had pledged $1 million as his portion of the costs. The legislature agreed to use the money in Sarasota. That was $4 million already, they figured, and they were sure they could get the land. I proceeded to look everywhere and was offered properties. Then the senator from Sarasota got in touch with me and told me we should put the theater on the Ringling Museum property because that, too, was owned by the state and it would be appropriate and, in fact, something he felt the Ringling people would welcome. Therefore the senator would not look kindly at going to any commercial place.

Negotiations started with the Ringling Board to see if we could arrange a contract to build a theater on their grounds but close to the Tamiami Trail, the front of the Ringling Museum. We went through five contracts that were unacceptable and I went through my own little hell to get the museum folks to be at least fair in what they were asking. They wanted control and they wanted everything they could get, thinking it was going to be a big thing.

In the middle of this, I hired a firm from England to do the architecture and they came to Sarasota. There was then a big controversy in the town. They did not want to see the old Asolo building, a lovely 17th century theater, exchanged for a modern facility that would spoil everything for which the Asolo stood. So they said we had to have something that would be quite like the old Asolo. I said, "My God, where would I find that?!" It would be too much money, even if we could do it, and it would be only an imitation.

There was a Scotsman in the group of architects and he said, "Well, what about a Scottish theater?" I said it had to be a beautiful antique theater. He said, "Well, there is a beautiful theater that was dismantled exactly the way the Asolo had been dismantled in Italy, and it was being kept as an antique, an asset." I asked him to inquire. It was under the control of the Scottish Arts Council (SAC). So he made overtures to the SAC and they, of course, said, "No way. We're not giving it to America." It was built in the late 19th Century and was a beautiful house.

I was thinking to myself, "What am I going to do?" I was wandering by the waterfront with Sue and, all of a sudden, I saw a tablet that said, "This tablet was erected in honor of the Scots who founded Sarasota." I almost went through the roof. The Scots?! I told Sue, we got a camera and I went back to this man and showed it to him. I didn't know, and I didn't think 99 percent of the population knew, that Sarasota was settled by Scots. "Oh," he said, "that would interest them." Well, then they wanted to negotiate.

So we went over to meet with the SAC and they had a lot of provisions. They had to send over their deputation from the Arts Council and we would have to put up a tablet saying this theater was from Dunfurmline, Scotland, and was the pride of Dunfurmline. We paid to have it shipped over and, indeed, started to work with it to put it into the space. Finally, a contract was agreed upon and we started to build it with the space behind it to do the taping.

We were proceeding and then two things happened that changed my life. One was the fact that Bernie Sliger called me to tell me that the lieutenant governor, who at that time oversaw the film committee of the state, was trying to develop

Florida as a film capital. The film committee members had come to Bernie and were very upset because they wanted a film school; they said this theater being built in Sarasota should contain a film studio and a place for a film school. The lieutenant governor told the president, "If you do this, we will give this school to FSU and I think it would be a great feather in Florida State's offerings. So Bernie called and told me to change it to a film school. I told him we'd already laid out everything and it would cost a great deal to change everything at this point. Nope, that's what he wanted.

Meanwhile, Burt had contracted some kind of illness, which the gossips of Hollywood were certain was AIDS. (Some of you may remember the great brouhaha when Rock Hudson came out with AIDS.) But Burt had been hit in the jaw by Clint Eastwood in a film they had made and his jaw wasn't broken but some tendon was damaged. It meant he couldn't eat or talk well and no one had an answer as to how to cure him. Obviously he was losing work, fighting the bad press and was in no position to deal with a film school or whatever.

I said to Bernie, "All right, if you want to do this. But I'm warning you we'll go beyond our budget." I went back to Tallahassee and met with the film committee; they had a huge space they needed to fill adequately to have a film school. I said building that would really raise the cost. I came back and gave it to the architect. He said it would cost us but they'd do it.

This got the committee on edge. They hadn't raised the money yet nor had they received the money from Burt. They told me to go to Burt and get his $1 million. I went out to California and he was in bad shape. He had lost weight and looked like he was seriously ill. And he didn't have the money. He said he had to give up two films. Unless he got this straightened out, employing him would be impossible. He told me he couldn't give the money now.

I went back to Sarasota and told the committee that Burt was ill and couldn't give the $1 million now. The woman who was heading the fund-raising committee accused me of talking Burt out of giving the money because the original plans had been rejected and they had added a film school. They claimed I was trying to sabotage the project because the original plan had gone down and I was striking back by getting Reynolds to withdraw his money.

I tried to get a call in to Burt, but his agent said Burt wanted *me* to explain that he was ill. I talked to Bernie and he said, "I think you'd better leave because there's strong feeling against you. Do you know what's happened?!" I said I had nothing to do with this. He said, "I know. Let's clear the deck." The woman who had made the accusation against me was appointed to the Board of Regents, so the university would not attack or question her.

I end this chapter by saying that my reason for making some of this part of my story is that, although I deeply regretted personally being pushed into this for money, I would look back and ask, "What did I do this for?" Well, I thought it would be helpful, and I told my wife this and I tell you this:

I know, had I not done this work with Burt for five years, the Asolo never would have continued because it would have had no home. Even though Burt never gave the money, he was the catalyst for the local people to raise money, which they might not have done without his name.

So, I say, yes, the state and FSU have a beautiful new facility that has been named the FSU Performing Arts Center and, therefore, was a result of Burt's idea, even though he didn't give the last $1 million.

I guess the point I'm making is, sometimes you make a sacrifice in your personal position professionally because, by making the sacrifice, you will benefit your theater or the university. The university got its chair, which it wouldn't have gotten; it got a beautiful theater in Sarasota, which it wouldn't have gotten; and it kept the Asolo, which likely wouldn't have been around—all of that even though, for me, it gave me much personal unhappiness.

I often have thought about it and have had to convince myself that those five years out of my life, and giving up the deanship and direction of the school were all worthwhile because of what came out of it. And you might say it was all worth it to achieve those things. But, in a way, does anyone now realize that occurred? No. Bernie is gone and no one knows what I had to go through. You don't look for praise; you look for results. In the long run, my vision of a professional theater attached to a university would have stopped had I not done this.

eight

Going back in time, I always was interested in the theater movements that went on in the period of the 1920s, '30s and '40s. These theater movements were significant because they resulted in the production of extremely important and successful plays, and they also were the seedbed for developing some of our distinguished actors and directors who were to become icons in the American theater. When I was in New York, I frequently went to 2nd Avenue to see the Yiddish theater company, which, at the time, not only had distinguished actors and directors but also evolved a "style of acting" that became something uniquely American.

Before the Yiddish theater and the type of acting that came out of it, most of the performances by actors and directors were influenced primarily by the British and European theaters. The British and European theaters were extremely interested in the speech, the dialogue and, in some cases, the poetry expressed by the authors. There was a development of styles that would fit everything from 19th Century comedies, to Oscar Wilde, to Shakespeare, etc. The Yiddish theater developed actors who had a tremendous passion, a tremendous energy. And, rather than concentrating on the delivery of lines, they concentrated on getting inside the characters they were playing and projecting an energy that was sometimes spellbinding.

This kind of approach made the theater at that point have a vitality that exceeded what was then practiced in England and other European countries. There was a dynamic that you could not miss. Many actors from that company went forth and began to practice that approach. Actors such as John Garfield, Paul Muni, Stella Adler and her brother Luther Adler were all part of the company at one time. Many went on to other theater roles on Broadway and many went on to the motion pictures and became known for their acting. The Yiddish theater was an extremely important element in the development of American theater.

So, at that time, I decided that the MacArthur Center would sponsor a series that would celebrate and recognize theater movements in this country. I chose the Yiddish theater as the first to be explored. I was amazed. Lewis Funk, who was editor of the theater section of the *New York Times,* was a friend of mine. He was very interested in the approach I was trying to take in celebrating these theater movements. He agreed to come in and become the moderator, as it were, of the discussions that went on with the members of these theater movements. When he and I approached some of the members of the Yiddish theater they were delighted because no one in New York or anywhere else had recognized or celebrated the contributions of the Yiddish theater.

Practically every member of the Yiddish theater came to Tallahassee. Herschel Bernardi came as the spokesperson for the actors in the Yiddish theater in which he had worked. It was an astounding program and we had discussions for two days. The students were invited to come in and participate.

The actors discussed how upset they were when the State of Israel was founded, it established the official language as Hebrew and did not welcome the Yiddish Theater people. I guess Israel felt Yiddish was an uneducated Jewish man's language. It was not the official language of the religion or the state. Now, at this time, I believe Yiddish is an accepted part of Israel and I hope they are doing some of the wonderful theatrical works of Yiddish playwrights. Everyone probably knows the best theatrical expression of this movement, which became an amazing hit—"Fiddler on the Roof."

Well, some of the people who came asked me, "How did you think of inviting all of us here? We didn't think there were that many Jewish people in Tallahassee?" And I said, "Well, I don't know. It's not because you're Jewish. It's because you have an exciting theater, which, indeed, set the style that became known as the American style of acting."

Then they came to me because they were so pleased and they asked: "Would you like to have us perform?" And I told them that would be wonderful, but I didn't know how the students would understand because some of it would be in Yiddish and some of it would not. I said, "Well, yes, that would be wonderful, because we'll get it on videotape; it probably will be something that hasn't been seen." They said, "No, we've not done this."

At first I was going to do it at our small theater, but someone came to me and said, "Oh, put it in the Main Theater." I was astonished again. We announced it was going to be a free performance given by the living members of the Yiddish theater. The house was packed. I never have seen such enthusiasm from the student audience as I saw in their reactions to these Yiddish performers.

I will give you one example that lives in my heart always. There was a man named Jacob Jacobs, who I'm sure was in his eighties at the time. He had performed in the Yiddish Theater and had done many things in vaudeville. He is noted by the song, "Bei Mir Bist Du Shön," which, of course, had been translated and was a popular song. So he came out on the stage, straw hat and cane, and did "Bei Mir Bist Du Shön" in English. Oh, they applauded him. This man was a typical vaudevillian and he had not received such applause in years, so he went off stage and then came on again, and then he went off stage and he came on a third time!

Well, Herschel Bernardi was backstage. After the third time through for Jacobs, with the audience standing up this time, Jacobs went off for the express purpose of coming back on again. Herschel grabbed him and said, "That's enough. Thank you!" But it was wonderful and probably was Jacobs' greatest experience in years because he hadn't been able to perform, and this audience was giving him a standing ovation. So he broke away from Herschel and did it a fourth time and

Herschel went out and almost by force took him off stage. But Jacobs had had the thrill of his life. He died about a year and a half after he appeared here.

The Yiddish style caught on because emotions were on the surface. Oh, you had no trouble hearing Jacobs. He would belt it all out like a trouper. It was so fascinating. And, of course, I used it as an illustration of how Yiddish theater influenced American acting. By celebrating this, I, of course, attracted the greatest of those living to be part of the first recorded history of theater movements.

The next movement I thought about was not a movement so much as it was a program to inspire the women students. It was called "Women in the Theater." I brought in a group of very successful women, including one of the leading producers in New York, one of the leading actresses, one of the leading African-American actresses and the woman producer who started the off-Broadway movement in New York. They came to illustrate to women, and to all of the theater students, that there was a fine place for women in the theater as actors, producers, directors and, of course, critics, because we also had the critic from the Chicago paper who set up "The Glass Menagerie," Claudia Cassidy. I think many of the women felt it was difficult to find work to equal the men because there was no doubt about it that most of the producers in New York were male. This proved that women could do so and that we had some very fine people here who did succeed.

The next theater movement I felt was important was the Mercury Theater. The Mercury Theater resulted from the days of the deep Depression that came to the country in the early '30s. The Depression not only affected laborers in their professional and personal lives, but it also affected actors and artists of all kinds. So Roosevelt set up the WPA (Works Progress Administration) primarily to put unemployed people back to work, doing what they normally would do professionally. For example, painters were employed to do murals in post offices across the land. And then they started the Federal Theater Project. This was designed to put actors and playwrights to work at the expense of the federal government. This WPA worked very well, but it ran into some of the problems that people feared in regard to the federal money that was given to the arts—which was censorship.

There were a number of plays written with a very communist tinge since many were turning against capitalism because of what had happened to cause the Depression. People were starting to feel that everyone could share and that the socialist system would be something that would equalize the wealth of the country. This resulted in so many rejections by legislators that it was decided the government would not allow these kinds of materials to be produced.

The first group to leave the federal WPA theater was the Mercury Theater, which probably became the most critically acclaimed theater group. It was engineered by Orson Welles and John Houseman. They staged a production of "Julius Caesar" in modern dress and it was an astounding work. They got a great deal of favorable press and people came to see their work. It became something where not only were they doing innovative productions, but the actors they assembled also were an extremely gifted group.

As it happens, the Mercury Theater lasted a few years before the people in the group began to get other offers. The first one of these, of course, was Orson Welles.

At that time Orson Welles was performing in the Mercury Theater, and in those days they performed on Sundays and were off on Mondays. Also at that time, Welles was playing the part of "The Shadow" on radio, which appeared live on Sunday nights. So he would have a taxi waiting at the theater door, race out sometimes in the costume he was wearing and go over to the radio studio. In just about nothing flat, he picked up the script and went on the air. He, of course, had a beautiful voice and on radio that became a very great asset. And he impressed everyone, even though he wasn't given credit for playing "The Shadow" on the program. Well, the radio producers decided, after the success of the Mercury Theater, that they could make use of him and offered him a chance to bring his company, the Mercury Theater, over to NBC studios. They'd become the "Mercury Theater on the Air," made up of most of the company actors.

So the company did a number of wonderful productions on radio and I'm proud to say I was part of one of them—not of the Company, but they did hire actors to do bit parts. Of course, the most famous production they did on radio was one that was a typical example of "in your face staging" for which Orson Welles and the Mercury Theater were noted. They did this program that was written many years ago, a story of creatures from outer space attacking cities, called "War of the Worlds." At that time, usually they would open the radio program by saying something like: "And now we present the Mercury Theater of the Air in a production of so and so and sponsored by so and so . . . ." What Welles did was to begin the program with: "Ladies and gentlemen, we now interrupt this program to state that outer space creatures have been seen landing in New Jersey." And he named cities: "Trenton is now under attack!" But it sounded like a real news bulletin. He started riots! People were taking their belongings and leaving the cities. They were looking up at the sky to see where these beings from outer space were. It created the biggest riot of people who were fleeing from what was coming over the radio. This happened mainly because it was done in a style that would hit them right in the face. It wasn't until the end of the program that he announced it was adapted from a work by H.G. Welles. And it was really that which led to federal regulations for what would go out over the air.

I had the Mercury Theater in Tallahassee and I got in touch with Orson Welles. He was in Europe, and said he had a run-in with Houseman and wouldn't come as long as John was there.

Well, it was an interesting program, an interesting series and the students learned a great deal about how that particular theater program influenced so many who went on to careers in film and so on, and what it contributed to theater in New York.

I next decided to do the Group Theatre, which was another theater movement in New York. Lee Strasberg and Harold Clurman were founding members. It was a theater that was put together at the time of the Depression by writers with a political slant, many of who made a statement on the condition of the working people and the stock market, which was mostly in the hands of the wealthy. Lee broke away from that and started his own school of actor training. I brought them into Tallahassee and it was because I was honoring the Group Theatre that I attracted everyone I could possibly contact. They were all people who had a great respect for Strasberg and the theater he developed.

I arranged an honorary doctorate for Mr. Strasberg while he was here, which he accepted. He said he had refused all other offers but would accept this degree because he respected what the theater school had accomplished by bringing the professional and educational worlds closer toward serving each other.

Lee Strasberg then did something he said he had never done before. He demonstrated with the students his technique in conducting the Actors' Studio.

Also at this time, Harold Clurman gave one of his inspiring speeches that brought him full circle in my professional life. I hugged him and said I was sure he had changed the lives of many of the students who had heard him as he had mine. Sadly, he died shortly after leaving us.

I decided to do a tribute to Milton Goldman, who was probably the leading actors' representative in New York. He was a very personable and very amazing man in his own right. He lived with a man by the name of Arnold Weissberger. Both of them traveled to Europe and knew everyone who was anyone in theater. Arnold collected a tremendous amount of memorabilia; he had original scripts by George Bernard Shaw among many other things. I had invited Milton and Arnold to come and be honored, but, unfortunately, Arnold died before we could bring off the tribute. But Milton did come and along with him came Helen Hayes, Lillian Gish and the remaining Andrews sister, Patti. It was one of the biggest groups of actors and entertainers he represented. I got the university president to give a special award to Milton to recognize his achievements. It opened up for the students avenues of understanding about the role of an agent. He set up the conditions by which he would see people, and he gave a clearer understanding of the business aspect to the students.

As you can see, I used all of these theater movements, which I thought were important, but they also gave opportunities to people who were affiliated with these groups to reminisce about and to come to celebrate. I found something these artists were interested in doing and which would bring them. Had I just said, "Come on in on your own," they would have charged a fee, if they came at all. As it was, they came happily because it was the only celebration of these various groups, which they all felt was long overdue, and no one had thought of this for them.

I mention this because sometimes innovative thinking and finding something of very great interest personally or professionally, can get the artist you would like to associate with your program, university, school or whatever. This was a magnet to so many of the people mentioned at the end of this book.

I should mention that Helen Hayes, who became such a stalwart friend, came to this campus five times. She was so struck with the fact that I had maintained a strong interest and devotion to her theater, meaning the theater of her day—all of these movements that were part of the development of theater of which she, of course, was a very active participant. Therefore, I was doing these things and they were all recorded on videotape, and some of them were sent to PBS. For example, when they wanted a study on Lee Strasberg, I sent them the tape. In other words, Helen came because she was being paid and also because she thought I was doing something important that she felt should be done.

Again, I illustrate this to say that these people were attracted because I found something that meant something to them and decided to do it. And they came because they, too, were interested and dedicated to participating in it. I mention this as a method—doing something for them that meant they did something for you. They came because they wanted to tell a story, and they did tell stories in many cases about these movements and how they started. I hope this is helpful in understanding how a wide range of gifted came to Tallahassee and became so important in helping students understand the theater.

nine

Granted, this little book is about me. However, it is not my life story. It is intended to give to young people entering the theater program at Florida State University or any university a path taken to find a mission in entering the Temple of the Theatre.

What is revealed is that, like so many young people filled with a desire to act and enter the theater, and who attempt to make a living by acting wherever jobs may be—in radio, television, film or on the stage—it started in a very selfish way to find satisfaction in acting for a living. The theater as an art form, possessing a vital mission to serve the audience as no other profession or art can, was not understood or even recognized.

The understanding of this mission can lead to finding different ways to serve the art and profession of theater other than acting. It may lead to José Quintero's own approach, that you do not do anything in theater that does not fulfill your artistic vision. He believed that your vision of the art of theater and earning a living may not be the same thing.

Whatever branch of the theater, all of the above applies. The demands and risks, as well as the possibility of not earning an adequate living, are always there.

To find your way, there must be mentors. I always have maintained that university training is primarily finding the mentors who will inspire, "light your fire," light your way to your place in the theater. You will treasure them your whole professional life. Seek them out from educational or professional theater.

There are fundamental qualities that you must acquire for any success in any branch of the theater. The first is Love. This does not mean trivial, changeable, self-serving love. Love, in the sense meant here, is placing yourself second to your fellow artists and placing the Temple of the Theatre above your own self-interest. Your main objective, because you respect them, is to serve the author, the audience and the students.

In the vital part of your career, which is making the right kind of friendships, I have some suggestions that have worked for me.

First, never approach an important and established member of the profession with the obvious and sole purpose of using that person to advance yourself.

As a very young, aspiring actor in New York, I had a true veneration for the theater artists. Therefore, I would try to meet those theater artists whose entire careers were dedicated to theater. I wanted to learn from them and I would offer to help them. I would offer to read with actors or help out a director or producer. My sincere admiration and desire to learn from older actors pleased them as the acting profession is very sentimental and enjoys helping young admirers. I befriended Eddie Dowling who soon considered me his son, and I remained so throughout his life. He sponsored me for membership in the Lambs Club, where I met and enjoyed the friendship of many of the great performers of the day.

The friends I made there and on my auditions remained. Many responded when I needed them. They were the true artists in the theater at the time. The experiences I have mentioned molded my approach to theater. The dear friends still live in my heart and guide me to this very day. Actors should know that words remain just words until they become thoughts that are endowed with a passion. I hope these words engender a thought that in turn engenders a passion in you:

"Keep in your soul some image of magnificence."
Robert Edmond Jones

"The Theater is a temple built by Man to reveal to an audience the true beauty of Man."
Harold Clurman

*"I am not in love with Life because it is pretty.
I am a greater lover than that. I find beauty even in
Life's ugliness."*

Eugene O'Neill

APPENDIX

Here is a partial list of those artists and theater professionals who have enriched the lives of students and faculty in Florida State University's theater programs as well as many community people. Each interacted with students in the classroom, in performance or in workshop. They illustrate the love for theater, for colleagues and for young people who are the theater's future by the finest, most dedicated artists and professionals in theater.

This list does not include Eminent Scholar Chair holders. NOT ONE OF THOSE LISTED RECEIVED ANY COMPENSATION EXCEPT HIS OR HER TRAVEL EXPENSES AND LIVING EXPENSES FROM THEATER OR STATE FUNDS WHILE HERE.

Honorary Degrees Awarded by Theater and FSU
Helen Hayes
Joe Papp
Burt Reynolds
Roger Stevens
Lee Strasberg
Audrey Wood

Actors
Adlers and Yiddish Stars
Dana Andrews
Maxine Andrews
Billy Barty
Herschel Bernardi
Vinnie Burrows
Barbara Cook
Ossie Davis
Ruby Dee

Eddie Dowling
Mildred Dunnock (Sarasota)
José Ferrer
Joan Fontaine (Jupiter)
Lillian Gish
Harold Gould
Julie Haydon
Helen Hayes
Celeste Holm
John Houseman
Barnard Hughes (son, Douglas)
Earle Hyman
Jacob Jacobs
Werner Klemperer
Vivica Lindfors
Norman Lloyd
James MacArthur
Kevin McCarthy
Ethel Merman (Jupiter)
Arnold Moss
Tony Randall
Burt Reynolds
Jason Robards
Martha Scott
Dick Shawn
Paul Stewart
Lee Strasberg
Susan Strasberg
Robert Urich
Eli Wallach
Efrem Zimbalist, Jr.

Playwrights
Paddy Chayefsky
Joseph Hayes
Sidney Kingsley (Pulitzer)
Gian-Carlo Menotti
Arthur Miller (Pulitzer)
William Saroyan (Pulitzer)
Maurice Valency
Mark Van Doren (Pulitzer)
Thornton Wilder (Pulitzer)
    (Sarasota)
Tennessee Williams (Pulitzer)

Directors
Harold Clurman
Jed Harris
Robert Lewis
Albie Marre
Lee Strasberg

Producers
Richard Barr
Cheryl Crawford
Jean Dalrymple
John Houseman
Albert Selden
Roger Stevens

Costume Designers
Millie Davenport
Pat Zipprodt

Stage Designers
Howard Bay
Sam Leve
Jo Melzener

Composers
Mitch Leigh
Giancarlo Menotti
Charles Strouse

Agents
Milton Goldman
Audrey Wood

Equity
Willard Swire

I humbly apologize to any whom I may have missed. Thank you, all.

Index

Y